"Sail Away" Photographed by B. A. F. Brehon,
Tangier Island, VA, August 2010

Anyone making disciples is reaching out to others on his

or her sea. Be mindful of how Jesus, the disciples, and Paul

reached out to others, sailing away from comfort zones.

Move outside of self to reach someone else for the Lord.

REACH ME WITH

SMILES

A Handbook for Developing Disciple Makers

BARBARA A. F. BREHON

WESTBOW·
PRESS
A DIVISION OF THOMAS NELSON
& ZONDERVAN

WestBow Press books may be ordered through booksellers or by contacting:

WestBow Press
A Division of Thomas Nelson & Zondervan
1663 Liberty Drive
Bloomington, IN 47403
www.westbowpress.com
1 (866) 928-1240

ISBN: 978-1-4908-3168-8 (sc)
ISBN: 978-1-4908-3169-5 (e)

Library of Congress Control Number: 2014905478

Printed in the United States of America.

WestBow Press rev. date: 03/25/2014

Dedicated to the memory of my parents,

Richard Thomas Fields, Sr.

and

Lillian Jerlean Watson Fields

Contents

Photographs by the Author

Bio Photograph

Foreword

Clearly, one of the central functions of the church is teaching. I have read more books on Christian education than I can remember. Some have been very helpful and quite informative while others have not been as informative. All claim to have a new twist on an old subject. The New Testament church took seriously the mandate of Jesus to disciple the world. In addition, this they did through their teaching ministries. Many churches give token consideration to the teaching function. One reason is the lack of resources that speaks to the very heart of the task.

I have known Barbara Brehon more than twenty years. I have watched God mature her into an outstanding Christian educator who has a deep passion and desire to do the will of God. *Reach Me with SMILES* directly addresses the weekly task of teaching the Bible in the local church. Reverend Brehon has years of preparation and practice in the ministry of Christian education, especially in the teaching ministry of the local church. She writes that the teaching ministry of the church should grow out of the needs of the congregation. A teaching church will become a magnet for new converts, nurturing and developing them into committed disciples of the Lord Jesus Christ.

Reach Me with SMILES was written by someone who is a practicing Christian teacher. It is written for everyday Bible teachers who want a tool that will improve their skills. Thirdly, it addresses the how-to questions. How do I start a lesson? How do I stimulate the desire to learn more about God? How do I motivate students? How do I involve those I teach in the lesson? How do I love the people who sit with me week after week? How do I encourage my students? How do I strengthen them for the journey of faith? *Reach Me with SMILES* will challenge, encourage, and instruct you in the fine spiritual art of sharing the Word of God with those who want to learn more about Jesus Christ.

As you read, allow the illuminating presence of the Holy Spirit to fill your mind and heart with new zeal for a great work!

Geoffrey V. Guns, DMin

Senior pastor, Second Calvary Baptist Church

Norfolk, Virginia

Prologue

Did you attend Bible classes as a child or teen? Mentally list the ways that you were taught as a child in Sunday school or a weekly Bible study, public or private school. Compare and contrast those practices to methods used today. Be sure to consider available technologies, strategies, and research about learning.

With these thoughts in mind, consider current practices in your church for teaching the Word of God. How is the Bible taught now? Is lecture the only format? How can a Bible lesson be taught in a way that will assist believers with spiritual growth? How can Christian educators reach students of the Word?

They can reach them with SMILES. Teachers who use this concept will **s**timulate, **m**otivate, **i**nvolve, **l**ove, **e**ncourage, and **s**trengthen believers. Believers come to the learning environment saying, "Make me more curious about the Word of God." "Help me to study the Word of God." "Keep me coming to Bible classes regularly." "Discipline me, so that I am able to practice what I am learning by seeing it in seasoned saints." "Lift me when I slip a little or fall." They also say, "Uphold me or be present with me when I am in need." Responding to each of these responsibilities would impact the educational ministry of the church. The chart that follows depicts the concept.

The SMILES Concept

TEACHER	STUDENT	IMPACT
S timulate	*Make Me* become more curious about the Word of God	Interest
M otivate	*Help Me* study the Word of God	Knowledge
I nvolve	*Keep Me* coming to Bible classes regularly	Inclusion
L ove	*Discipline Me* so that I am able to practice what I am learning by seeing it in seasoned saints	Model
E ncourage	*Lift Me* when I slip a little or fall	Reconciliation
S trengthen	*Uphold Me* and be present with me when I am in need	Energy

The primary focus of *Reach Me with SMILES* is to answer one question: How do you teach a Bible lesson that will assist believers with spiritual growth? SMILES is an acronym that will help you improve existing teaching skills. The SMILES concept recognizes that Christ is the center or focus of all teaching and the learners are the second priority. Teachers deliver the Word of God to their students so that they grow or mature spiritually. To assist believers with spiritual growth, use SMILES.

Using the SMILES Concept

SMILES can be incorporated into teacher development or training sessions, focusing on one aspect at a time. Weekly, monthly, or quarterly intervals depend on the needs of particular groups. I recommend monthly sessions to allow time for practice and self-evaluation. Teachers can interact with one another to review progress at general meetings regularly.

An overview of the SMILES process and review of the aspect being emphasized takes place at the regular teachers' meetings. The leader facilitates discussions so that the teachers' strengths become building blocks and weaknesses are improved with the support of the team. Teachers use SMILES with all church auxiliaries and committees regardless of their age. When the teachers and learners blend or mesh, the impact is phenomenal. (Review the chart.) I have used this approach in urban and rural churches, in a juvenile prison, as well as in all levels of public and private education. It was also effective when I taught preachers in a seminary.

As the teacher **stimulates** learning, students become interested and curious. When the teacher is motivated and **motivates** the learner, knowledge and wisdom increase because the Word of God is studied. As a teacher teaches the students how to study the Bible, believers will sense that the teacher is a disciple, also. With intentional **involvement** of all persons in a class session, the attendance becomes more consistent or steady. For example, in a typical setting, the enrollment may be twelve to twenty persons, and the average attendance might be five to nine students weekly. Attendance, at a glance, may not be encouraging. However, when you take time to look at the frequency of an individual's attendance per month and dialogue with them about their personal study, you may find that the learners are still in the Word weekly for personal devotions, growth, and study. We cannot separate the tie between motivation and involvement. Their involvement creates a desire for more. Are they studying the Word even when they are not with you?

Furthermore, one of the best techniques for reaching someone for spiritual growth is by modeling the desired outcome. The teacher leads by demonstrating the preferred behavior (such as Christian **love**), and the learners practice the biblical application in their everyday lives. The result will be Christians becoming reconciled to the Lord through the teacher's encouragement and continual affirmation walking together in the way of the Word. When life becomes bumpy along the way, the teacher **encourages** the learners; the teacher lifts them by reminding them of the living hope that is found in Jesus. (1 Peter 1:3-4).

The final stage in the development of the SMILES concept is to **strengthen** the learners, giving them the energy to press on in Christ. When we hold up the bloodstained banner of Christ, we uphold the learners in whatever condition they present themselves. We are present with them when they are in need. As this process plays out, reciprocal relationships are built. The energy emitted from a group that has learned to demonstrate SMILES has Christ as its power source.

Using SMILES will help disciples become more effective disciple makers. Disciple makers are Christians who have consciously decided that they want to not only strengthen their personal relationship with Jesus but also help others to grow. The disciple maker teaches others to not only follow but also study the teachings of Jesus to become more like him. *Reach Me with SMILES* is designed to help you spur persons who work with you along a pathway that is Christ-centered and other-centered. The SMILES concept will help disciples become more effective disciple makers. Effective disciple makers either assist a nonbeliever or encourage a believer to move toward Jesus. Either may be sitting on the pew beside you, singing in the choir, ushering, or participating in various ministries in the church. Effective disciple makers are able to teach people to develop a better relationship with Jesus. Sharing the Word of God with those who want to learn more is exciting and will keep you smiling.

Becoming a Teaching Church

The direction the church takes to become a teaching church must be based on the needs of that congregation within the community it serves. Teaching is one of the two most important ministries of the church. (The other is preaching.) The goal of teaching is to improve the quality and effectiveness of Christian living and win others for Christ as stated in the Great Commission. (Matthew 28:19–20). Church members should grow because of the teaching ministry. The maturity of Christians can be effectuated through a diverse teaching ministry under the leadership of a visionary pastor. In addition, whether or not a church is progressive and willing to make changes will affect its future. Therefore, Christian education must continually assist the members of the congregation with envisioning new images that keep the individuals focused on a biblical pattern for living. For example, following the Beatitudes found in Matthew 5 will equip believers for daily living.

Building Visionary Leadership

Visionary leadership and well-chosen resources can effectively move a church into a dynamic and relevant future. When we consider what is relevant, we must realistically recognize that relevance means different things to different people within the same church. Think about what makes something relevant or meaningful for you. *What's in it for me? How will it help me?* Leaders must address these questions as they relate to current circumstances, which change. Everyone's answer may be different depending on his or her station in life at that time. Over a period of time, the same person's answers will change. We must meet the needs of people where they are. We must remain relevant. The attitude of the leadership in any church will affect the altitude of its teaching ministry.

The term *leader,* used here, refers to the pastor in particular, but also any person serving as head of a group within the local church. That could include the minister or director of Christian education, the superintendent of the Sunday school, anyone who teaches weekly Bible study, presidents or chairs of committees, etc. The spiritual height of a church largely depends upon the degree of emphasis the leader places on teaching the Word of God. When you consider the average weekly schedule in your church, how much time is allotted for teaching? In comparison, how much time is given to rehearsals (choir, ushers, praise dance, etc.)?

The leader must keep the vision before the church. Where the church is going should be lifted higher than where the church has been. Though tradition is important to the vitality of a congregation, it must be tempered with the needs and direction of the membership. The congregation has to be taught that they can go beyond where they are in order to realize their potential. Certainly, we can do more than our own past, since Jesus said anyone with faith in him would be able to do even greater things he did. (John 14:12). Therefore, leaders must be intentional about teaching the people how to praise God. Praise nurtures hope and commitment to the kingdom's work. It is not good to minister for maintenance; instead, keep a dream, a vision, out front to take the congregation beyond where they are. Develop a how-to teaching style.

Revisioning with Purpose

The teaching should center on building spirituality and faith in order to serve the people in the community. It should allow opportunities for the learners to express their condition of existence and a praise of God in view of their circumstances. Application of what is being taught should be the focus; it is possible that the church will need to revision and train with intentionality. Teaching should be purposefully directed toward a specific, desired outcome. Envision what that will look like. It should be deliberately planned in ways to ensure that impressionable Christians are not easily persuaded by false doctrines, as stated in Ephesians 4:14.

Moreover, pastors must realize that evangelism brings in new members with their own ideas regarding what the church should be. In order to keep the membership—seasoned and new members alike—working toward the same goals, teaching must be intentionally planned to reshape the old as well as to mold the new.

The process of developing a church's new vision or tweaking an existing one should be shared between the pastor and the congregation to allow a sense of ownership by all. The greater the sense of ownership is evidenced in the majority of the core leaders within the congregation, the greater support and participation there will be. People are more likely to work toward a goal they helped formulate. However, focus on the crucified Christ who ascended into heaven should never be compromised.

When a church leader revisions, care must be taken to make the process meaningful for the people. It is important to use familiar language and updated worldviews. Diverse life experiences should be engaged so as not to limit the intelligibility of biblical, historical, and theological meanings for the average person. In other words, people are different. Engaging them requires diversity so they are given multiple opportunities to learn. Individuals understand best through varied teaching and learning styles. Leaders must provide opportunities and sources for meaning that answer the questions the people are asking, since the people are in pursuit of faith. Leaders or teachers should avoid using too many examples of their own life situations that occurred during the week. While sharing personal testimony and experiences with the divine in your weekly routine is of critical importance, overemphasizing personal concerns can hinder the participation of others. Those who continue to come will not come expecting the opportunity to share their experiences. People receive greater meaning when they participate in the process of teaching and learning. When teachers realize during a class session that theirs is the only voice being heard for an extended time, the teacher must pose appropriate questions to encourage more student participation. Teaching must be student centered—more Christ and congregation, less you.

Using revisioning to create meaning for people will result in a higher quality of living for God. This could mean establishing a full weekly schedule in lieu of programs and meetings on Sundays. Even in your personal life, your schedule reflects your values. Pastors must promote teaching and learning in order for their congregations to cherish the value of Christian education. A church has to be taught how to be in relationship with God; Christians are not born knowing. In Joshua 4:6–7, the Israelites are told to inform their children what the stones meant to them, thereby passing on, or teaching them, how to be in relationship with God. Therefore, the ministry of the church should be organized around worship, teaching, and missions rather than separating them.

In Matthew 28:19–20, we learn that the goal of teaching is to make disciples. Intentional instruction keeps the vision of the church in view. Consequently, the members must receive training in what missions involve, how to do missions, how to evangelize, how to study the Bible, how to worship, and how to pray. Teaching in the church that is concerned about its future involves the establishment of an ongoing vehicle for growth in all of these areas, evidenced by higher levels of service encouraged by the leaders. In support of this idea, Apostle Paul says we should entrust to reliable persons, who will teach others. (2 Timothy 2:2).

Mediocrity is not acceptable when it comes to teaching God's people. Do not just grab anyone to have a warm body filling a slot. Since teaching is a spiritual gift (Romans 12:6–8; 1 Corinthians 12:28–30), it is simply not acceptable to entrust teaching the Word of God to those who are unqualified. A person who has no relationship with the Lord is unqualified to teach a Word they have not personally accepted through salvation! That creates a recipe for stagnation rather than growth.

Recruiting and Cultivating Resources

Besides visionary leadership, appropriate resources can effectively move a church into a relevant future. Relevance for the people must be dynamic or lively rather than static or motionless. One of the most valuable resources of any church is the people themselves—the teachers and the learners. It is an arduous task to keep co-laborers focused on God and rework a church's educational structure at the same time. The goal is improving the quality and effectiveness of Christian living to win others for Christ. When workers are enlisted, the goal must be kept in mind. Recruit and utilize teachers who not only possess the spiritual gift of teaching but who also are also skilled in facilitating the discovery of a believer's connectedness to the biblical text. To do this, the teacher must show fruit, evidence of knowing Christ as personal Savior. (John 15:8). Christian educators must teach for meaning that reaches the learner through relevance to the learner from the selected scriptural text. Teachers must avoid lessons that center on teacher or current events with no connection to the text.

Accordingly, teaching in any auxiliary in the church should invite learners of all ages to explore their own views as compared with those found in Scripture. Teaching should prepare persons for life outside of the walls of the building, so that they can fulfill the Great Commission. Then, the learners will be enable to take the lesson with them for application in their daily lives. Since people experience and define reality differently, the individual learner should be the focal point of the teaching as compared to the teacher.

Next, the relationship between a person and culture must be addressed. It is important that Christian educators be open-minded, flexible, and willing to change in order to reach the learners for

God. When I think about developing a teaching church, a vital consideration is a group of committed and dedicated workers who know God through the saving grace of Jesus Christ. Persons recruited to lead or teach must have experienced a connectedness of their own to the Bible. Moreover, Christian education goals and ministries cannot be maintained without adequately trained, experienced, and visionary core persons.

I can hear someone saying, "But you don't understand. We can't find enough people like that." My sincere response is that it is better to have one dedicated, sincere, and seasoned saint teaching one larger class than to have unbelieving, fruitless family members slowly killing the body of believers. Christian Bible teachers must be believers themselves. No, no one is perfect. However, we have a right to expect those who teach to be reliably qualified to teach others (2 Timothy 2:2). Also, consider John 15:8 telling us that we show our discipleship by bearing much fruit. Christians have a spiritual right to hold church leaders accountable.

Choosing a Teaching Design and Curriculum

A particular design for the teaching church should be selected that enhances the goals of the church. The **developmental** teaching approach embraces a curriculum that encompasses various stages of development. Religious, moral, emotional, and cognitive development should be considered when choosing a sound curriculum. Christ-centered materials are a necessity for Christian teaching. These materials emphasize morals that are Bible based. Even when we insert pieces of our ethnicity, we must lift persons who possess Christian character traits. In addition, concepts and activities in the curriculum should encourage students to probe introspectively with age-appropriate discussion questions. Tapping into emotions does not have to be any scarier than tapping into the mind for cognitive (intellectual) growth. Recognize the need for the materials to address the whole person or be ready to use the teacher as a human resource. The teacher will compensate for the areas not addressed in the curriculum. What did we do when there was no money to buy books and many people were not able to read or write? The teaching design should not only be developmental but also **life centered**. The Scriptures suggest a sequence to life, and the teaching design employed by a church should intentionally optimize the motive behind all teaching in the church.

If the teaching or curriculum is not relevant to the students, the participation in the church's teaching opportunities will decrease and become stagnant. It is imperative to make a connection from ancient to contemporary times. One way to do this is by presenting the *kerygma* (life, death, resurrection, and ascension of Jesus) for personal identity using tradition and Jesus stories. The aim of the teaching, then, is focused on spirituality rather than instruction for instruction's sake. Students must be helped to make life decisions based on the Christian story. Reflecting on positive and negative contemporary stories as compared to Christian stories encourages the learner to make a link or connection from their current life situation to a parallel story in the Bible. Teachers must facilitate those experiences with creativity and flexibility rather than relying on lecture alone. People need to be liberated from their present states of existence, and the teaching process is more meaningful as well as more effective when it connects to the needs and interests of the learners.

Moving Forward

Several directions should have an impact on teaching for a dynamic and relevant future. Ministries should be based on meeting religious needs as the priority. Many people who move from church to church and new converts alike seem to be looking for the same thing. They appear to be in pursuit of faith. A strong teaching ministry and commitment to discipleship would send people out to do ministry, providing opportunities for those on faith quests to experience lifestyles of faith.

To do this, the congregation must be able and willing to change in some respects in order to grow. This progressiveness should encompass a move from low expectation to high commitment communities of faith; low quality to high-quality ministries; Sunday program emphases to seven-days-a-week schedules. This progression should go from limited teaching to extensive teaching, from dull and boring worship to exciting experiences, which are not necessarily measured in decibels. Move from modest missions programs to missions organized around teaching and worship. Rather than organize around "doing good works," focus on feeding the spiritual needs of the membership. Progressive leadership and appropriate resources can effectively move a church into a future that is dynamic and relevant to the people.

Major problems of any direction chosen by the leadership to become a teaching church would include volunteer and untrained teachers as well as inadequate curriculum. Before embracing a particular direction, a Christian educator should be careful not to ignore theology. Education with comprehensive goals does not compensate for theological value. Having information is one thing; the method of presentation toward the goal of the Great Commission is the other integral part of effective teaching.

In order to be considered a teaching church, there needs to be a commitment to growth. Since learning is a lasting change in a person brought about by experience, Christian educators must be concerned about spiritual growth. Those experiences provided by Christian education should be underscored with spiritual formation to help individuals grow and should not isolate individuals from the issues of the real world that they face daily.

Summary

- The direction the church takes to become a teaching church should be based on the needs of that congregation within the community that it serves.

- The *attitude* of the leadership in any church will affect the *altitude* of its teaching ministry.

- Leaders must keep the vision before the church.

- The teaching should center on building spirituality and faith in order to serve the people in the community.

- Applying what is being taught to daily life should be the focus.

- Pastors must realize that evangelism brings in new members, who bring their own ideas with them regarding what the church should be.

- The process of developing a vision, or revisioning, should be shared between the pastor and the congregation to allow a sense of ownership by all.

- Intentional instruction will keep the vision of the church in view.

- A church should select a teaching design that enhances the goals of the church.

- One of the most valuable resources of any church is the people themselves—teachers and learners.

- Teaching in any auxiliary in the church should invite learners of all ages to explore their own views and those found in Scripture.
- Both the teaching and the curriculum must be relevant to the learner.

Stimulate

Reach out to me.
Stimulate my interest. Make me become curious about the Word of God.

Stimulate

How do you teach a Bible lesson that will assist believers with spiritual growth? Believers come to us for instruction, saying, "Reach me by stimulating me." We must remember to glorify God always as we attempt to stimulate others. When we stimulate others, we provide an atmosphere that evokes a desire to want more—a closer relationship with God, more time in studying the Bible, more intimate worship, and more time in service to others in the name of Jesus.

When people come to church or to a Bible study of any type, they expect or anticipate spiritual stimulation. People were created to be in relation *with* one another, not in isolation *from* one another. Why is solitary confinement within a prison considered a severe form of punishment? The importance of stimulation is at the root of the answer. This suggests that our teaching should not isolate. People who are depressed, deprived, depraved, disadvantaged, or at risk have something in common: a lack of stimulation in their environment. They do not come so that they can leave in the same state of mind they were when they entered. The most effective Christian educators are those who are sensitive to creating learning environments that provide the proper stimuli for the specific needs that people bring. Would daily lectures with no other style of presenting information be acceptable to the parent of a public or private school student? Would you be satisfied with a child in this century being lectured to as the only means of receiving information for each year of their formal schooling? Adults are *children* of God too.

Following are some specific practices teachers can use to stimulate believers in God's Word.

Cultivating Deliberate Disciples

2 Timothy 2:15 tells us that we must study. If our churches are going to be the churches that God intended, we must be intentional about preparing for this responsibility. As Christians, we are commanded to make disciples of all nations or to teach all nations. Teaching is a spiritual gift of the Holy Spirit, and we are obligated to nurture or develop it so that it can be used to the fullest potential in Jesus' name.

Ultimately, everything we do must glorify the Father and edify the body of believers. Consequently, the role of the teacher is to make disciples of others. Disciple making refers to what we do to assist others with spiritual growth while discipleship is personal. Are you growing? Are you in position to stimulate life-long learning and lasting spiritual growth in others?

Christian educators must want to attract and disciple non-Christians while we grow closer to the Father ourselves. Our discipleship causes us to witness to persons who have not yet accepted Christ as their personal Savior. The same Christian, or disciple of Christ, must also want to be an effective disciple maker of persons who have made a profession of faith in Christ. What does the disciple do to assist other disciples with their spiritual growth? Is this not deliberate or intentional teaching?

Deliberate disciples expect to increase in Christlikeness, thus coming closer in relationship with God. As we seek to provide Christian nurture to others, we recognize a need to learn methods that are the most effective for ministering to the souls entrusted to us. Therefore, the person who educates Christians helps others to grow in such a way that they are formed in the very image of Christ. Since pastors are Jesus Christ's under shepherds, ministry leaders are "under under shepherds." How does your ministry nurture souls?

Rediscovering the Joy of Teaching

The joy of teaching comes when you see the light of understanding overcome the faces of students or when you see changes in their talk. The joy comes when the quality of the discussions is eagerly and equally engaging week after week. The enthusiasm in believers is matchless after you have spent hours preparing for them. Understanding that joy is a fruit of the spirit, we must also acknowledge that the fruit of the Spirit must be developed in order for us to live in the spirit (Galatians 5:22–25). One way to develop your joy as a teacher is to prepare appropriate stimuli for the believers you teach. Failure to prepare adequately can cause dryness in your teaching. When the teacher becomes complacent and satisfied with the same methods and procedures, the students tend to become bored; the energy and excitement of learning slowly dwindle, and the joy is lost.

A practical education philosopher, John Dewey, said that if there is no learning, there is no teaching. He was concerned with the whole person in a total situation. He did not believe that authoritarian, or strict, methods offered contemporary people realistic preparation for life. He saw learning as problem solving. The person

"…cannot get power of judgment excepting as he is continually exercised in forming and testing judgment. He must have an opportunity to select for himself, and then to attempt to put his own selections into execution that he may submit them to the only final test, that of action. Only thus can he learn to discriminate that which promises success from that which promises failure; only thus can he form the habit of relating his otherwise isolated ideas to the conditions which determine their value."[1]

If this was stated at the beginning of the previous century (1903), then it is certainly more relevant in this age with so much technology abounding.

The implication for a Christian educator is no different. Become a more effective teacher by developing a better understanding of the people that you teach. Learn to manipulate the environment, not the Word of God. Help students to get in the habit of testing their judgment by putting faith into action, and rediscover the joy of teaching.

Insisting on one teaching style for all learners does not work very well. When we recognize the value of the experiences of others, we accept the importance of believers comfortably participating in a variety of learning activities without having to use extreme methods of coercion. I cannot make you what *I* want you to be; however, I can provide opportunities for the Word to show you what God is saying about your situation in life. I will not be aware of that situation if I use only one method or style of teaching that does not allow time to hear from you. The teacher as facilitator stimulates discussion groups. Discussion groups focus on the message or concept that the lesson lifts up for a given week. The point is to make sure that believers walk out knowing what Scripture has to say about a particular issue or concept raised from the passage of the week or stemming from a concern a student raised during the discussion. If we never intentionally posture the lesson to hear what is relevant to them, we will not likely address questions they need answered that came up during their week. Change, or growth, as a process will have been facilitated with the Holy Spirit as the energizer when we expect and anticipate their sharing.

Moreover, the Christian educator must emphasize more than processing information, even when the information is biblically based. God allows access to information, technology, and anything else; everything in creation is for his glory. Stimulation can sometimes occur simply by varying the structure of the learning environment. That could be physical, emotional, and/or spiritual. Teachers, then, may have different responsibilities than previously perceived, not fewer. Consideration must be given to more than cognitive (thinking) processes. Gestalt teaching suggests that learners perceive as a whole and respond to the basics that seem significant to them. (*Gestalt* is the German word for "form" or "configuration.") The form, format, or delivery style of the teacher's lesson must accommodate individual differences. If you do the same thing the same way repeatedly, not much will change. Christian educators want lifestyle changes.

Creating an Atmosphere for Growth

Would you continue to attend a class that was cramped or too hot all the time? Location and physical comfort play a vital role in creating an atmosphere that is conducive to spiritual growth. Would you want to keep coming to a place to hear a message of hope when you are in a packed-like-sardines room while the room next door is larger with a lower attendance? Would you want to know more about Jesus when you are sitting in a cold place with your arthritis flaring up? Step out of your comfort zone and ensure that the room is conducive to the needs of the students. I understand that some church facilities do not have "classroom space" for every level and use a portion of the sanctuary for classes. The same concepts still apply. When you think of a comfortable environment, several things are suggested: luxury, contentment, sufficiency, tranquility, rest, relaxation, or nourishment. In addition to the biblical information that is presented, Christian educators address any or all of these factors at one time or another as we attempt to reach others for Christ.

What would be the best location for a class attended mostly by senior citizens or toddlers, teens or middle-aged adults? When a group outgrows its space, reassign locations to ensure a comfortable environment. While it is important to be organized, it is also important to understand the need for flexibility. Furthermore, it is good to have more than one plan that considers the needs of the people. People get used to "their" class meeting in a certain place. Before changing a location, show consideration for others by informing them of the impending move and the rationale behind the move. The mind needs time to relocate as well. By allowing for mental adjustment time, a better idea may spring forth.

According to educational research, both experience and perception play a role with the learning situation and the learners' expectations of themselves. In churches, the people will not necessarily participate if their attitude toward the stimuli is negative. People voluntarily attend church. We do not have a captive audience but rather a group of individuals who choose to be a part of the local gathering. We must learn techniques that stimulate people to want to know more about the Lord by placing value on who they are as created by God. Learning, then, is facilitated by prior experiences of the learner. Learning is based on insight and a series of discoveries. In other words, learning by doing is key, and effective teachers must structure the teaching-learning situation so that learning is stimulated. When believers are stimulated positively, the teacher's joy increases.

Meaningful conversations that emerge in class are well worth the effort expended to create the atmosphere for table talk. The depth for class discussion comes from the prior preparation of the teacher along with the presence of the Holy Spirit in the lives of the people present. Christian teachers use the presence of the Holy Spirit, and their knowledge from preparation and experience, in addition to consideration of those who will be taught. Skillful teachers carefully craft phrases to draw out of believers whatever the

Holy Spirit needs. The combination creates a portable concept for the students. Ask questions and present information to point to one key concept (not more than two) per week. It is simpler and easier to redirect students' "talk" toward the central idea of the week in this way. Keep in mind that it may take a little time to get a group used to the idea of not being lectured to week after week. I am not advocating the abandonment of the lecture method. However, it becomes less critical that the teacher makes each point prepared on the paper. The most important thing is that the believers walk out with at least one spiritual concept to guide them and redirect their thoughts toward life-altering habits.

Discussions provide opportunity for clarifying personal beliefs. The classroom atmosphere enables the Holy Spirit to create confidence, which is needed to fight the battles of day-to-day living. The teacher can assist believers' spiritual growth by allowing opportunities for them to articulate their thoughts, knowledge, and feelings. Learning that others have similar concerns and hearing how they handle situations stimulate the believers' spiritual drive and fortifies their resolve to stay on the battlefield for the Lord. They can receive that from a gifted teacher; however, the application is stronger when multiplied by other persons in the class.

Barbara A. F. Brehon

Asking Questions That Stimulate Discussion

Deductive approaches allow less rigidity and more flexibility. When teachers ask deductive questions, they are moving students from the big idea to smaller ideas. This way, different general statements of explanation, hypotheses, can be formulated. They are tentative interpretations of complex ideas or biblical truths. Deductive questioning allows learners to discover the truth as they explore the logical consequences of a hypothesis. Better questioning techniques give details to students and use a step-by-step approach at the same time. Develop a series of prepared questions from the concept or premise of the week. Let the questions lead the participants toward the suggested behavior or attitude that comes from the Bible lesson. The teacher is not the one to initiate the statements of truth. Leading questions are prepared that goad the believers along. For example, let us say that the scriptural lesson is taken from Romans 10:14–17. The concept of the week can be that faith grows by listening to God. The deductive method may begin with a scenario to illustrate the truth of the week followed by a series of questions. The teacher may choose to ask the questions prior to reading the Scripture to stimulate the lesson.

Deductive Questions for Participants
(from the Big Idea to Smaller Ideas)

1. What is faith?

2. From where does faith come?

3. Give an example of how growing faith is demonstrated. Be sure to use words that describe specific observable actions.

4. When is the last time God spoke to you? What did he say? Where were you when it occurred? Spend this week reading at least one verse from the Bible. Then, sit still for a moment. Write down your thoughts after you have been quiet for a while, thinking about the verse. Your thoughts during this time may tell you what God is saying to you.

Imagine the excitement that can be generated when believers *uncover* biblical truths as compared to being told those truths with little time provided for them to wrestle with it.

On the other hand, **inductive** questioning provides the hypothesis or the biblical truth. When teachers ask inductive questions, they are moving students from smaller ideas to the big idea. A generalization is a concluding statement that represents a tentative solution to a problem based on available information at the time. The teacher may use this approach to pinpoint a specific truth that is the focus of the scriptural lesson.

Activities and discussions are developed that draw this hypothesis or biblical truth out of the believers. For example, the concept of the week from Romans 10 is clearly stated initially by the teacher. "Faith grows by listening to God." The Scripture would probably be read early in the lesson. The teacher may pose questions, such as these:

Inductive Questions for Participants
(from Smaller Ideas to the Big Idea)

1. Tell us about a time when you listened to God.

2. Share with the class an experience where you did not consult God first.

3. What are some things you can do to improve your ability to hear God?

4. What verses in the lesson today will help your faith to grow more this week?

No rule says that you have to approach each lesson the same way. Let the theme of the passage or the concept of the day determine those specifics as the Holy Spirit directs you. Discussions that lead to self-reflection tend to cause believers to spend more time outside of the class sessions reading and rereading the lessons. They like the way it makes them feel from the inside out and want to have something to contribute when given another opportunity.

Inquiry teachers lead discussions with questions that stimulate or energize the conversation. Feel free to ask spontaneous questions that stem directly from current conversations on the floor. However, only ask questions to which you really want to know the answer. You will be able to show that you care about the students. There should be no "devil's advocate" questions in this teaching strategy. Instead, the teacher could use the question stems, such as these:

- What led you to say that?
- What evidence in the Scripture supports that idea?
- Show me where you see that.
- Do you agree that …?
- Do you agree with his point that …?
- Student 1, tell Student 2 why you disagree with her opinion.
- What do you mean by that?
- Why do you think he did that?
- How is that? When is that the case? Why is that?

Facilitating through Small Groups

Most of us regularly run out of time to cover the points that we want to emphasize each week in class. Facilitating small groups within the class is one way of increasing time for discussion. Asking poignant questions and giving students an opportunity to wrestle with those questions stimulates spiritual growth as they seek biblically based answers. Choosing the best question for a specific lesson requires that you consider the meaning of the passage of Scripture being studied and the contemporary issue to be addressed or resolved. Plan at least four questions to centralize the discussion on the topic of the week. Moreover, it is natural that other questions will emerge as the lesson is presented and believers begin to interact.

Small groups are usually safe places for everyone to share experiences or concerns. Believers who need more support that is spiritual gain it by participating in small groups. The teacher as facilitator not only keeps the discussion groups stimulated but also redirects believers when they stray too far away from the concept being emphasized. For example, you could say, "I didn't think of it that way. Tell us how that is connected to growing faith (or whatever is the theme of the week)."

Bonding, caring, trusting, and inquiring are products of the time spent developing this approach to teaching the Bible. It takes time to cultivate it. Just as God gives us time after time to get our relationship right with him, we need to invest the necessary time to stimulate our students. As the needs of believers are met, life-altering decisions can be made. After all, we want a lifestyle change that leads others to Christ. When believers see the Word lived out in the lives of the teacher and other people in the class, a lively hope exists that makes it attainable for them too.

Creating Images That Stimulate Growth

I challenge Christian educators created in the image of God to use knowledge for God's glory when teaching God's Word. Many believers could comprehend more if they were taught to use images based on experiences. The idea of using illustrations is certainly not new. When our teaching gets stale, though, images can be refreshing. Images that occur to the teacher while privately reading sentences in the Bible should be used to illumine the lesson to be covered. These images or mental pictures are portable. The picture is worth more than a thousand words.

How do you create images that stimulate? Show the believers how they can take the pictures created in their minds with them for life application. Talk about how the image came to you and how it made an impact at a specific time for you. One caution: as you share of yourself, keep it brief. The apostle Paul is an example of one who made a point using himself, but he kept the details to himself. We still do not know what his "thorn in the flesh" was.

"Thorns," Jerusalem, March 2003

However, we do know the biblical truth that Christians must not be conceited or self-exalted (2 Corinthians 12:7). Let us look into a rationale that further supports this approach.

B. F. Skinner, well known for behavior modification techniques, suggests that behavior is influenced by what learners say in inner speech. One can change behavior by helping them change this inner dialogue. The implication is Bible teachers would provide biblical models for learners to imitate. For example, point out the rewards for the character read about in a particular passage. Paul is one biblical example, just mentioned, that illustrates a model teachers can use for sharing personal testimonies. To employ the implication from Skinner, the teacher would provide reinforcement when desired change is evident. Be aware that you saying it does not necessarily make it happen for somebody else. You can know the change in the believer has occurred from personal testimonies, not supposition, judgment, or just because you said it. Offer support to reinforce the changed behavior and give demonstrative praise to God in class for the evidence of that change.

There are other implications for Christian educators who know that God created us in his image. We know that each of us possesses innate abilities that are uniquely crafted each time God chooses to form someone in the womb. According to educational research, the right brain controls a portion of our personality. Right-brain thinkers are more creative and not necessarily verbal. This research is not new. This 1970s model of brain systems has been updated to include eight brain systems.

- linguistic—use of language
- logical—use of reason
- spatial—use of the body (the person) in relation to other things around it to get the big picture
- kinesthetic—use of the sense of touching
- musical—use of creativity of expression
- interpersonal—use of relationships between two people

- intrapersonal—use of relationships with a broader range of persons outside of the group
- naturalist—use of the environment

How can the average teacher of the Bible use any of these or any combination of these methods to develop a theme or a biblical truth?

1. Consider the idea that poor readers are better at relational thinking than analytical thinking.

2. Consider the possibility of asking, "What if …?" after teaching or "How did it make you feel?"

3. Imagine the creativity of people who are nonverbal or quiet.

4. Show the geography of the passage in a concrete manner from time to time.

   a. Simply use a map. Have a large one available rather than telling them to use the one in their Bibles. (Students may not have maps in the Bibles they brought with them.)

   b. If someone has traveled to similar places, let them share.

   c. Show pictures using the computer and LCD projector. There is so much available software.

5. Clustering or grouping details helps learners visualize the big picture.

   a. Spatial ideas require intuitive or divergent thought and are holistic.

b. Find the emotions or the gutsy experiences in the lesson. Explore them with prepared questions. Do students find them accepting, visionary, or only a dream? Referring back to educational philosopher John Dewey, give students the chance to test their judgment that can be later applied into action in a personal sense.

The right brain can also synthesize the left-brain information in a gestalt (very structured) versus holistic manner. In other words, one side of the brain structures information. Remember earlier it was stated that gestalt teaching suggests that learners perceive as a whole and respond when it is significant to them. When we present whole forms, we use gestalt strategy. Part of your brain can figure out information the other part receives.

The gifted teacher recognizes that there are differences in the proportions of either mode the students use to process information or to learn. The gifted teacher does not try to figure out who learns which way best. The Holy Spirit handles that. The teacher simply varies the presentation style so that various modalities are used, letting the Spirit dictate that while planning and presenting. The likelihood is that more people will be reached with the diverse stimuli. The main theme of this whole book is reaching others to grow God's Kingdom. Dare to sail into the students' waters.

Some thinkers are verbal, relational, and analytical. They may have rational, logical thought. This may create linear thinkers who may need outlines. People with these tendencies may appear to be critical or all knowing. The Christian educator stimulates the thinking of *all* believers for Christ. You can predict some believers to be realistic, authoritative, scientific, or conformist. Do not let this pose a problem for you. Patterns of reasoning can develop from the Scriptures as you let the Holy Spirit tell you what questions to ask; the Holy Spirit can reach every type of thinker in the room. There are times to be a relational facilitator, and then there are times when logical sequences need to be integrated. Ask the Holy Spirit to guide you through that.

Know that learning is individualized. You cannot learn for me any more than I can learn for you. Nevertheless, *if* I could teach you, couldn't you learn? Then teach as if you know it as truth.

Points to Ponder

- Pray that the Lord will show you how to stimulate *all* of his people that you teach for his service. He knew them when he formed them.
- Examine yourself and pray for God's guidance for lesson planning.
- Use measurable and universal language for the people you teach.

- Choose words that are easily understood by all. Our word choices must draw responses that allow the participants to see the Lord at work in their own lives.

- Teach to each one.

- Warning! Individualized teaching may increase your preparation time.

Practice

- Read Psalm 139:1–18, 23–24.

- As you communicate with God through Jesus Christ, do the following:

  o   Examine yourself.

  o   Consider themes or concepts and then choose one or two.

  o   Think about modalities that help people learn.

  o   Plan a lesson that uses multiple modalities.

Sample inquiry method based on Acts 1:1–14

(v. 4–5)   Do you recall an experience of leaving a place and wishing you had stayed a little while longer? Share it.

(v. 6–7)   What might happen if you got something back that had been taken away from you, such as a house, jewelry, job, or spouse?

(v. 7)   What would it really be like to know everything?

(v. 8)   What two things must you know?

(v. 9–11)   How do you stop fixing your attention on inappropriate things? What is your sky?

(v. 12–13) Where do you have to go to go back to your Jerusalem (to wait on the Holy Spirit mentally and/or physically)?

Responding Responsibly

In order to keep believers stimulated, be aware of the responses you give as well as the questions that you ask. Value statements you make can harm the hard work you put into planning the session. The trick of the enemy is to have you unaware of judgmental things you say. For example, a student has just finished speaking and you say, "That's good." Somebody else had previously articulated something and you did not really say anything; you just went to the next part of the lesson. This person may wonder if you thought something was wrong with what they shared. Hers was "good," so mine must have been "bad." It is certainly not your intention to judge anybody. However, a weaker mind may perceive it that way as Satan tries to enter. Remember even the strongest Christian has weak moments. To use language that judges their answers or statements as valid or invalid may quench the Spirit of God.

- Avoid thinking in terms of right versus wrong.
- Focus the conversation on the text being read.

- Remember to be a teacher who facilitates and inquires.
- Remember to allow conversation that does not center on the teacher.
- Prepare questions in advance.
- Avoid answering the questions you ask. Wait a moment and give them time to reflect on what you are asking. This stimulates dialogue with God.
- Erase the impression that the right answers must come from the teacher.

Learners may not value what the teacher's point of view. Teacher responses can be questions. How can you phrase an appropriate question that redirects the thinking and refers believers back to the Bible, back to God? We can reach believers in three domains or areas.

1. Affective (emotional)—how does it make you feel?
2. Cognitive (intellectual)—what does it make you think of?
3. Psychomotor (behavioral)—what can you do to show ...?

Recognize that God reaches people spiritually. Teaching is often cognitive, or mental, without spiritual emphasis. The teacher's focus is getting through the information prepared on time. No wonder people dropout and stop coming. To counteract this, conduct quarterly self-evaluations and class valuations. **Evaluation** is the individual's judgment of himself—students and teachers alike. A **valuation** refers to something of value, what it is worth. Is your teaching valuable? Is there evidence of the movement of the Holy Spirit in the lesson and their lives?

Paul wrote in 2 Corinthians 13:5 to examine yourself. Evaluate yourself. Give students the opportunity to express their opinion about their growth, study, and progress as well as the process used to teach the class. How do we know if there is learning if we do not build in assessment strategies? What we do to determine our own effectiveness as teachers should not prohibit growth. What we do must enhance the growth of individuals for Christ. *Warning! Do not ask if you are not ready to hear the answer and do something about it!*

Understand that each person in any class is operating at a different level. Spiritual, cognitive (intellectual), affective (emotional), psychomotor (behavioral), social, economic, and self-esteem are all levels that vary. The variations are not only from person to person but also within any one person. No one has a high, medium, or low level of all. Your format or content at a given time may be inappropriate or not on the proper level for someone. That one sheep or the group needs diversity to attain and retain your point. Use techniques to reach everyone with different levels of questioning. How do you determine the appropriate level for any of the areas mentioned? Keep it simple. Ask the questions that you want answered.

Many things point to being an inquiry teacher. Avoid asking questions for the sake of asking. Avoid giving the impression that you do not want or care about their answers. Do not produce inappropriate information or judgments regarding the people you teach. Respond responsibly. Think of it like this: teaching in the church does not provide captive audiences. When the natives get restless or offended, they flee. Consequently, the teacher may be left with fewer and fewer people in attendance. Devil's advocate questions have no place here. You are not the devil's advocate, and neither are your students.

Turn the learners into discoverers; make them ask you to tell God's story (Joshua 4:19–24). Show the geography of God's glory. Today he can move in our lives, his territory, in the same way he did in ancient times if we trust his leadership and obey his commandments. If God says do not do something, then don't. If God says do it, then do it. If God says not at all, forget it! (Joshua 11). Let the Lord have his way.

How do you teach a Bible lesson that will assist believers with spiritual growth? The teacher should stimulate, motivate, involve, love, encourage, and strengthen all believers. Stimulate learning so the learner becomes interested and curious about the Word of God. When a student is stimulated, there is an apparent attitude that says, "Make me want to know more about the Word of God." The impact for the teacher who receives this attitude would be the interest of the student in continuing to be a part of that teaching-learning situation. The teacher should stimulate all learners regardless of the age of the group. When the teacher and the learner mesh, the impact is phenomenal.

Developing Teaching Techniques

The most effective Christian educators merge how to study the Bible with how to apply it in daily life. Effective teaching techniques emerge as the Holy Spirit births freshness in your planning. While you are teaching, intentionally use words that show what you do when you read and study the Bible. Use the words *observe, interpret,* or *apply* and then break down their meanings:

Observe: *What does the verse actually say?* You might ask the students to identify words that name people or ideas, words that show action, or words that express emotion. What did the person do or what does the verse say that God did? The point is to get into the wording of the text.

Interpret: *What did that verse mean when it was written?* Consider the person who wrote it. Then consider what it meant to the people who heard it or read it. Explore the context of the verse or passage. One way to pull out particularities of context is with PERCS, which stands for the political, economic, religious, cultural, and social dynamics prevalent at the time of the writing. When the

Bible student considers a combination of these factors found in the text, deeper understanding of biblical truths results.

Apply: *What does the text mean today?* Now is the time to transport what it said and what was happening then to contemporary thoughts. Bring the life of the reader to the discussion. There is much discussion of how to make application in the pages to come. Application is the core of *Reach Me with SMILES*. Christian educators who model concepts taught are most effective.

- Let learners know that you care enough to let the Holy Spirit uncover how they learn best. Stimulate each other and rediscover the joy of teaching.
- Present information and concepts in ways that challenge the learners to think for themselves.
- Show students how to read the Word of God and communicate with God while in private personal study at home.
- Make the learner ask for more.

Martin Buber, another icon who influenced educational philosophy, developed the thought that **dialogue** confirms both participants as having unique value. These mutual relations give students confidence to think for themselves. By engaging students in dialogue, a teacher as facilitator can lead believers to choose between alternatives. The Christian educator should likewise assist believers in becoming active conversationalists with classmates and God, never closing their minds or hearts while seeking more profound truths than they already possess. It does not matter how spiritually mature they are; everyone can always find something they never reflected on before.

Stimulate the conscious by using all the senses. **Tactile** experiences are those things that require the sense of touch. There are times when the lesson becomes more alive because the teacher gives the opportunity for the believers actually to touch one another to express care and compassion. Another way to use touching in a lesson would be to have objects that represent ideas. For example, feeling the fuzz on a peach during a discussion on the fruit of the spirit would be a reminder that others see what is produced when you grow in the Lord. Persons who are not verbal learners remember object lessons longer.

Kinesthetic teaching provides the use of other senses jointly. How many of the five senses can you use to demonstrate or illustrate one concept or biblical theme? A combination of hearing, touching, seeing, smelling, and tasting can be used in many lessons to avoid the strict lecture-delivery method. Shift gears in teaching; give them something different in tone (activity). Hook teaching to muscles and music. Make students move to point out a topic. Illustrate the topic through song. Teach problem-solving skills rather than providing the answer to every question you raise. Ask them to demonstrate what they would do if they were a character in the lesson. Give them the opportunity to plan then role-play it. Allow discussion that lets the observers share feelings and images that were invoked while listening.

Know that imagery is creative imagination and allows people to visualize while they read or paint a mental picture after reading. Teach in a way that gives learners opportunities to describe their imagery. This gives them the chance to share how they feel about situations in life and make appropriate responses when faced with similar situations in the future.

Invite believers to compose and envision their own knowledge. Give believers opportunities to clarify their thinking and challenge one another's thinking. Allow them to teach each other while "the teacher" acts as facilitator of the process.

You could dare to have adults actually draw or paint a picture—yes, even adults—in order to stimulate discussion. Put into pictures what cannot be put into words. Rejuvenate them with word associations, clustering, or webbing to generate relationships. Many of the believers we teach could effectively assist us, since some of them have used a plethora of techniques at their workplace or in school.

It is obvious that the ideas presented here will not work well without some degree of student preparation. They need to read and study prior to coming to class as well. They need to take notes actively or journal the thoughts the Holy Spirit gives them outside of the class setting. They might just do that if they know that they will have opportunities to share and ask questions in class sessions. The most inquisitive believers become your helpers, and care should be given when organizing small groups to avoid putting the inquirers in the same group. Try becoming an inquiry teacher and rediscover the joy of teaching.

Applying Christian Teaching Techniques

The effective teacher is a steward of God's time. Time management and lesson planning include prepared questions, activities, projects, etc. It includes a variety of approaches to learning coupled with enthusiasm. Get fired up about studying. Grow in grace with planning. Recognize that your personal study time and planning time are separate entities. Let the Holy Spirit control the climate of your classroom, and stay fired up about teaching with diversity. The sky is the only limit!

Use a theological approach with a variety of techniques. **Theology** is the belief system or faith stance that guides your convictions. It is the study of God and godly things. As a Bible teacher, you must be aware of a personal position with the Word and how the Holy Spirit is able to manifest itself through that Word to reach people for God. Thus, a theological approach is one that begins with faith that Jesus will guide you to the specific delivery style that is needed to reach the people who will be present that day and in a particular context. That process begins with the teacher; the preparer's heart must be pricked and pierced by the Spirit of God.

Some churches use a specific curriculum that provides the lesson aim and have a staff person, the pastor or designee, who reviews the lessons in teachers' meetings. This does not excuse the teacher from personal prayer, moments of meditation, and time-consuming table work required for executing God's plan. Spend time considering the background and general characteristics of your students. How do you teach a Bible lesson that will assist believers with spiritual growth? Incorporate them and their needs in planning and delivering the lesson. Students know how they learn best; hear them.

Differentiating Instruction

Are there students in your class who repeat everything you or their classmates say? Though it may become irritating at times, realize its probable purpose. Perhaps they are **verbal** learners who need to mouth ideas themselves to be certain that they have grasped them. Prepare specific activities to capture the verbal student in a way that does not hinder the class. If you know that oral or outspoken persons will be present, plan for them in a manner that meets their need. Be aware of verbal learners being literal thinkers. Avoid using **rhetoric**.

Using clichés, jargon, popular phrases, or examples because they seem to fit does not add to the exposition of the Bible. If it comes out, that's one thing; just be aware of how you are using language. Rhetorical statements or examples that you use may be taken literally or exactly as you say them. Because believers come to class at different stages of spiritual maturity, it is difficult to determine when a common expression you use may be taken literally. This further supports that variety in your teaching style or technique is needed. More people are reached in their context when a variety of approaches is utilized.

Some believers are not quiet by nature, but in class, they will not speak up. They sit quietly rather than participate actively. They may be learners whose dominant learning style is hearing or **auditory.** They listen to and thereby seize the acoustics of the context. They need to sit back and absorb all that goes on like a sponge. From time to time, they will speak out for clarification, having apprehended in part. When the teacher is **person minded** while planning lessons, the need to blend auditory, verbal, and visual methods of presentation is apparent.

Some people are good with their hands. As they explain what they are trying to say, they have to have their hands to shape it. They can make things and do things with their hands that amaze us. They probably learn best that way, too. **Kinesthetic** learners are those who need to make contact with a concept. If they could literally handle it, they would understand it or grasp it more quickly. How can we get students to touch something that represents the main idea of the lesson? What can they hold? The Holy Spirit will answer as you meditate. Realize that using illustrations goes beyond pictures with words. Representations or icons help people to perceive truths of God more clearly sometimes than words. What images come to mind while you are studying, and how can you use available resources to depict them? Who in your class needs to see something in order to make a personal connection? How can you show them what the Scripture of the week says? The Spirit of God will answer as you take time to meditate.

Many things have analogous relationships; two things can be compared that are not normally associated with one another. Such comparisons appeal to **visual** learners because they are ocular people who need to be able to see it for themselves. *Ocular* refers to people who benefit most from illustrations, diagrams, charts, and the like. The teacher must provide experiences where concepts can be observed. The teacher uses phrases from the text to show similarities or likenesses and differences. Comparisons are used as symbols that allude to our Christlikeness. We have been created differently but in the image of one God; we try to imitate his Son so that we can someday be with the Father. It is fitting to use imagery and symbols or objects to represent the concepts in the biblical lessons that we teach. Jesus did. When preparing a lesson, take the time to pray for the Holy Spirit to show you which image to demonstrate. Remain focused on the one, not more than two, concepts for one week.

Imagine one lesson, the concept of the week, one verbal technique, one auditory method, one kinesthetic form, and one visual image. When presented in one block of time, more of the persons present will be reached for Jesus. Of course, not all of these may apply to the lesson at hand each week. Nevertheless, I urge you always to utilize differentiated instructional techniques. People learn best in a variety of ways. The point is that our teaching style should reflect an understanding that God created us differently and we are required to teach his Word to all of his people.

Practice

Use Matthew 5:16 to identify a teaching technique you can use in a lesson plan for your students.

Apply as many of the following modes as possible to guide your thinking. They are presented in random order.

- dialogue
- tactile
- kinesthetic
- theology

- verbal

- auditory

- person minded

- visual

Summary

The most effective Christian educators merge how to study the Bible with how to apply it in our lives. If we can do that, effective teaching techniques will emerge as the Holy Spirit gives birth to freshness. You teach people; you teach people the Bible with Jesus as the center of the lesson. What is it about this young lady or this gentleman, boy or girl, that I need to reach today for Christ? Did I feed him or her today? Last week? Will I feed them with the lesson that I am preparing now? How do I make it portable for them?

- Develop an atmosphere that is conducive to believers such that they feel free to be expressive without being judged.

- Be intentional about having time to build relationships with each lesson.

- Let the lessons draw students out rather than drag them along.

- Use materials to accentuate or give emphasis to the lesson.

- Meditate daily, paying attention to any images revealed by the Holy Spirit.

- Practice reading the Bible for yourself *before* reading it to prepare for teaching.

- Become an inquiry teacher who uses inductive and deductive reasoning with appropriate questions.

- Know that learning is individualized.

- Become a more effective teacher by developing a better understanding of the people you teach.

- Learn to manipulate the environment, not the Word of God, and rediscover the joy of teaching.

- Remember that when believers are stimulated positively, the teacher's joy increases.

- Prepare questions and presentations to point to one, not more than two, concepts per lesson.

- Understand that it may take a little time to get a group used to the idea of not being lectured to week after week.

- Structure lessons so that believers will walk out with at least one spiritual concept that will guide them and redirect their thoughts toward life-altering habits.

- Keep believers stimulated. Be aware of the responses you give as well as the questions that you ask.

Practice

Reconsider a basic Bible study method: observe—interpret—apply. Use it as an outline for various stimulating techniques to deliver a lesson. Before you plan the lesson for others, make it personal.

Identify God's plan in each passage below. Choose one to develop into a lesson. Concept: Jesus had a plan. Do we?

Acts 1:4–8

Galatians 4:1–7

Ephesians 1:3–10

For Further Reading

Anderson, Lorin W., ed. *International Encyclopedia of Teaching and Teacher Education.* Pergamon, 1995.

Armstrong, Thomas. *Multiple Intelligences in the Classroom.* Association for Supervision and Curriculum Development, 2000.

John Dewey. *Ethical Principles Underlying Education.* University of Chicago Press, 1903.

Orlich, Donald C. et al. *Teaching Strategies: A Guide to Better Instruction.* D. C. Heath, 1980.

Yount, William R. *Called to Teach: An Introduction to the Ministry of Teaching.* Nashville: Broadman and Holman Publishers, 1999.

Motivate

Reach out to me.
Motivate me to want to know more. Help me study the Word of God.

Motivate

How do you teach a Bible lesson that will assist believers with spiritual growth? Believers who come to us for instruction are saying, "Reach me by motivating me." When a teacher is motivated and motivates learners, knowledge and wisdom increase because the Word of God is studied. Instructors show learners how to study the Bible, and believers can sense that the teacher is a learner as well.

Delivering Lessons That Motivate

Teaching for learning is a process. An effective teacher knows what he or she is teaching and why it is being taught. Goals are set specifically to enhance the Scripture at hand. Christian teachers teach to enrich lives for Christ and to emphasize results based on a Christian theological approach. A Christian teacher knows how to draw the most out of believers through a variety of techniques as they reach the ultimate goal of reconciliation and relationship with God.

Varying teaching techniques give believers multiple opportunities to use the lesson to help someone else. Therefore, time management and lesson planning are very important to guiding a person with spiritual growth. It takes time to identify age-appropriate activities that focus on the one message a lesson will bring out to a particular group of believers. The art of asking questions is critical to a good lesson with meaningful discussion. Projects for all ages can be discerned so that the learners can make it personal and take it home. Using intergenerational and cooperative lessons from time to time helps believers to become connected to one another as they learn to connect with Christ. If these activities and projects are service oriented, imagine the bigger benefit of ultimately reaching others for Christ!

Now, let us assume that your church is a teaching church. This means that teacher effectiveness is increasing and the teachers are personally prepared to teach the lesson. One part of lesson preparation that may often be overlooked is for teachers to visualize or imagine following through with the lesson before it is actually taught. Imagine the following:

- You arrive early enough to set up the classroom for the lesson.
- You arrange the chairs to accommodate the day's activities, since they will vary from week to week.
- You write the lesson outline on the board or place the Post-It on the wall with the outline on it that you wrote at home. You place the first transparency on the overhead projector, ensure that the LCD projector and computer are ready, check that the appropriate maps are displayed, etc. Teachers with classes in

the sanctuary may have other concerns, though I have used these methods in sanctuaries.

- You set up material, props, or resources you will use before believers arrive, so that you are mentally available to be person minded with believers as they enter.

- As students arrive, have them begin sharing about their past week as general conversation. Only two people may be present at the time, but start by talking about the week. There may be a testimony, praise, or a personal struggle; things may come up that need to be spiritually handled. Intentionally allow this time at the beginning of class weekly, so that needs and concerns do not have to travel around with the students or the teacher for another week.

- Take the opportunity to make a connection to the previous week's message conversationally, and go into the lesson of that day. In addition, class always starts on time. The conversation is part of the class. Students may want to get there so they do not miss anything.

- Create an atmosphere where students feel comfortable bringing any reaction to your attention that may be left over from the previous week and needs can be addressed.

- You may use prayer as the official beginning of the lesson; however, it does not have to be the first thing on a facilitator's lesson plan. Conversation is an important transition into teaching the Word.

As this becomes a routine, some believers will look forward to the time of sharing and become more punctual. As the facilitator becomes more person minded, a sincere concern to know who these people really are and what they like to do emerges. Who likes to go fishing? Maybe some of them can get together and go fishing sometime. You cannot fish in your classroom, but look at the relationships that are being built while on the pier or on the shore. Have a fellowship outing to the movies. Alternatively, you may have the class over to your house for a fellowship meal or dessert. Choose a person who may be naturally suited as a fellowship leader to be responsible for organizing a quarterly outing. People feel included and develop a commitment to the class. Christian bonding and nurturing will develop.

If you are really teaching, you are trying to effectuate or facilitate a change in the believers. Consequently, teaching in the church should invite learners to explore their own views and those found in Scripture. That does not have to happen in the church house. Enabling the learners to take the lesson with them and apply it to their daily lives results from the time to explore their thoughts as they reflect on scriptural lessons. The relationship between a person and his or her culture can be addressed and those who have been on a faith quest, needing new friends for a new lifestyle, will begin to feel victory in Jesus. An open-minded and flexible facilitator is willing to change in order to reach the learners for God.

Think about how you teach the Bible. Didn't Jesus socialize? He was often at a celebration. He worked hard on the Father's behalf and went on retreats. Do you remember that he stopped by Mary, Martha, and Lazarus' house? If Jesus took time like that, why shouldn't we fellowship with believers? We are not Jesus, but we are trying to be like him. We have different gifts, abilities, and interests; we are individuals who like to go to different places. Until we become like Jesus, we will work on his behalf with what has been given to us. In the meantime, we will work toward the ultimate goal. When we get to be like him, we will go to be with him face-to-face.

Once the informal discussions at the start of the class have taken place, the facilitator makes an appropriate transition to move into the lesson. Be cautious not to spend too much time talking about current events, such as news stories and politics. Bringing them up is not so much the problem; staying with those topics while students came to hear and share from the Bible can frustrate the students into not wanting to come on time. By the time they arrive fifteen to twenty minutes late each week, they are present for hearing the lesson start. Whether all the information prepared is covered is not more important than the people feeling fulfilled and complete when they leave on fire for the Lord. When this happens, the teacher has done the job for the week, even though the plan may not have been covered in its entirety. The lesson was delivered not only with a connection to the previous week but also with relevance toward the one message that came out of the Scripture of the week. The Holy Spirit took charge.

Do not force-feed or overload the students. Give believers the amount of information mixed with application that they can carry out of the door with them. Teaching Sunday school or weekly Bible study isn't like grocery shopping. When you shop for groceries, you can buy many bags of things and carry a trunk load home with you. When you get to your residence, you can go back to the car as many times as necessary until you take all the groceries inside. Give people an opportunity to reflect and receive within their souls what they can bear. Now, they can use it when they walk out. Focus on one topic or theme per lesson and develop it using as many different activities and discussion enhancers as possible in the time frame. Do not frustrate the soul with too much at one time. They may stop coming, continue a faith quest elsewhere, and choose to be fed by someone else because they experienced no victory.

Reinforce one point at a time. Pause intentionally, taking twenty to thirty seconds of silence so that the Holy Spirit can let that Word sink in. Let a thought sit with people instead of rushing to the next point because you have a schedule to keep. The most important thing is that believers get what they need for that week. The next week, don't try to play catch up with what you didn't cover. It is not *your* show. You can assume that believers are keeping up with the reading and studying at home. You affirm their participation. As you go on with the next lesson, remember that the time at the beginning of the session can conversationally tie up loose ends. Some re-teaching may need to take place.

Another approach is to start by presenting information and lead to the lesson aim. Provide time for shared experiences and very brief testimonies of the past week, and then ask a simple question. It could be the lead to the lesson. For example, suppose the discussion from the previous lesson asked the relevant question, "What are you really all about?" The next lesson could begin, "As we talk about our lesson today, I really want you to consider what you are all about." Remember last week's lesson was framed with that question. In a sequential study (a series of lessons from a specified curriculum), the teacher may add variety from ending with a question by beginning with one. Students receive the connectedness and are more readily prepared to be engaged from week to week.

Yet another way to initiate the session could be with someone reading a selected verse or short passage aloud from as many different versions as are available. Have students summarize what it says, what it meant in the biblical context, and what it means to them. Of course, the remainder of the session leads them toward the concept that has already been carefully thought out and prayerfully considered by the prepared teacher. If reading from only one version, you may wish to decide which version more easily captures believers who did not read the lesson before the class. The King James Version is popular, but it is not necessarily the easiest to understand. Making your point and moving on to the next step in the process for that week sometimes flows more easily with other versions of the Bible.

I have found that some people in the congregation believe that the King James Version is "the right" one to use because it is the "authorized" version. What they don't realize is that the king of England in the 1600s authorized the Bible to be translated into a language approved by the English church authorities. A faction within the church, the Puritans, had problems with the earlier translations. The "Authorized King James Version of the Bible" was contemporary in the 1600s as compared to the fourth-century Latin Vulgate translation of the Bible from which it came. Since then, God has enabled others to translate the Word into language that can be understood in contemporary terms. Recognize that the use of a word changes over the centuries, even in the same language. Since most of us are not able to read Hebrew, Greek, or Latin, the best way we can rightly divide the Word of truth is to read multiple versions of

English translations. The Holy Spirit then helps us to know what God is saying to us today. That's exactly what King James authorized so many centuries ago.

There are times when the teacher can lead believers through a sequence of questions, pausing appropriately for reflection. Such times do not necessitate believers verbalizing their answers. The teacher simply makes sure that believers go through the process of thinking. Presenting a series of carefully thought-out questions is one way the teacher can lead a class in a particular direction. The teacher ensures that they go through each step outlined in the lesson of the week.

Different lessons lend themselves more to certain techniques. You can recapture images that occur while you read and study the Scripture as you design or develop your methods for delivering the lesson that week. You may think of particular music and have the CD, smart phone, or iPod players to share with the class at the appropriate point in the lesson. Individuals in the group are great resources for creativity. Think of their particular characteristics or skills while you prepare. You can call the person during the week and ask them to do something specific for a couple of minutes when called upon during the lesson. For example, ask two people to share an experience that addresses the theme. On the other hand, ask them to bring a particular object that illustrates the lesson and give them the opportunity to explain its significance to the lesson. Explore different things to do as the Spirit gives you the image. What is the thing that you like to do and how can it be incorporated into an activity to enhance a scriptural concept? Ask the same question as you consider gifts, abilities, hobbies, etc. of your class.

Choosing Appropriate Resources

To develop a concept from Scripture, use electronic databases (computer programs) and search for key words. Topics that are spiritually identified for your teaching can be cross-referenced in this manner for a meaningful and in-depth study. Computer programs are relatively simple to use and some are available in public libraries at no cost. Simply go online. There are also a number of books shelved for your use in public libraries. There may be a seminary or school of theology in your area; utilize that library but realize you may not be able to borrow materials overnight. Plan to spend a couple of hours browsing these resources.

Motivating Teachers and Learners

I believe that people want to be taught. "Help me to study the Word of God so that I gain knowledge of God's will for my life." This statement could be the cry of a student or leader. I asked myself what motivates me to read the Word and study to teach it. My first answer was that I want Jesus to be pleased with me. I actually like reading the Bible and I get pumped up as I prepare to teach or preach God's Word. It is not a laborious task; it is a joy. I like word studies. I truly get pleasure from journaling thoughts and rereading them weeks later to see God's pattern for working in my life. I have found that it motivates others when I share how God speaks to me. It helps them to recognize the manner in which God usually communicates with them. It is wonderful to know that my way is not the only way. Hearing how God talks to others encourages me to be attentive to other ways he may show up for me.

Conversely, there are times when I become discouraged and have little zest for the depth of preparation that is needed to feed God's people. A poster I read once said, "No one ever said teaching is going to be easy." What do I do to power up again? Once when that happened, I asked the people in my class what they needed from me. I felt confident in the relationships that had been established to solicit the help I needed from the ones who would benefit from the boost I needed. I asked them to tell me how they learn best. I asked them what approach I needed to take for the lessons. During a class session, I let them know that I was becoming a little frustrated and I needed them to help me to know how to plan for them. The result was that they answered me. Someone said that they needed something like a study guide with questions they could answer. Another stated they enjoyed the existing format and admitted that they were not investing the needed time. A commitment was made to do better. Still others wanted a better understanding of the connections between the Old Testament and New Testament. What are the blood relationships between and among biblical characters (genealogy)? They wanted to continue allowing discussions of the concepts in the lesson. Their answers invigorated me.

None of their responses was new. They had shared them at various points before, but I needed a refresher. The Holy Spirit helped me to reopen myself. If I teach them every week and pray for them regularly, why can't I expose myself to them? They knew me just as well as I knew them and probably already discerned that something was amiss. Hearing from them triggered a renewal of my spirit. It was like a revival. Talking to, listening to the persons in the class motivated me, and reinitiated the zeal to continue the journey with them. In not so many words, we recommitted ourselves to studying the Word of God together and holding each other accountable to being prepared for class sessions. This took only a few moments before going into the scriptural lesson of the day. Subsequently, new faces began to appear in the class and the people who promised to come back did. The regular disciples demonstrated that they were disciple makers; they shared their enthusiasm about studying the Word of God with others and the class grew from the inside out.

Teaching is indeed a gift of God. It is an honor, a privilege, and a joy.

Points to Ponder

What drives your teaching? Discover what motivates you.

What role do others play in motivating you to be that way?

How would you define the relationship that you have with your class or your staff?

Take a closer look at what may set them aglow. How *do you* teach a Bible lesson that assists others with spiritual growth?

How do you motivate others to want to learn more about God?

Motivating Learners

You can expose biblical truths in such a way that the door opens for learners. You can give them opportunities to explore their thoughts in connection with what the Scripture says about particular issues. You can allow them to have experiences with others, sharing how God manifested himself in their lives. In other words, Christian educators must be intentional about allowing believers of the Bible to participate in discussions about particular issues they have experienced as reflected by specific biblical accounts of similar circumstances. However, you can only do so much; the individual has to make the decision that it is time to grow.

A Christian educator inspires others of any age to want to learn more by acting as a conduit to conversion experiences. To be a conduit to conversion, you must know your role as a facilitator. You are like a means of expression for them. You are God's instrument through which the Holy Spirit passes to activate the desire to want more of God and godly things. The activities, images, discussions, etc. that are shared in classes act as change agents. Students apply the concepts to their lives and can make decisions that draw them toward God's will. Illustrations make a difference—age-appropriate visual aids make concepts portable for participants. Facilitators motivate believers to live what they are learning.

Once a person has made the decision to follow Christ and seeks the knowledge of God's Word, the teacher serves as the activator who facilitates experiences with the Word. The experiences must be student centered. The facilitator shows how certain passages have helped others and gives witness to what Jesus has done personally for them. "If he did it for me, he'll do it for you." The teacher does not have to do all the sharing. The learner is impelled to share their stories and become participants in life-long spiritual journeys. Remember to utilize various modalities of learning discussed in the "Stimulate" chapter. There are so many ways to make the lesson portable.

The teacher, the conduit, is the medium through which the Holy Spirit conveys messages from God. God speaks through every participant; however, the responsibility of transmitting the message in the class setting rests with the teacher. The Christian educator serves as a temporary communicator for the Lord, who conducts the learner through canals in life. You conduct them until they feel the power surge and connect themselves to the power source on a continual basis. When a learner becomes the carrier, the teacher knows that motivation has taken place. However, the Christian educator and the learner cannot stop there, for it is a never-ending process. You become co-laborers who not only motivate each other but also spread the Good News to still others. We need to spur each other to continue in the faith.

How do you urge someone to want to grow in Christ? You cannot, but God can. The Holy Spirit is a marvelous friend. When we depend on him to guide us, we can do all things that lead to a closer walk with the master teacher. How did Jesus reach people for the Father? He started where they were and showed them truth and love. There is no law against sharing the truth. Galatians 5:22–25 tells us that if we belong to Christ, our ungodly desires and passions have been crucified. We bear the fruit of the Spirit and there is no law against that. Paul motivated people to live and walk in the Spirit. Christian educators today can create an atmosphere that compels Christian growth. Make them want to know more by showing them the truth and believing that they can have a transformed and victorious life with the Lord. Be authentic and experience real joy. Learn how to exercise your spiritual gift and appreciate the spiritual fruit. Deliver the Word of God to learners so that they mature spiritually and do not remain dependent on the teacher.

You may be in a nighttime experience in your teaching, but know that joy comes in the morning. Motivate the learners by remaining self-motivated.

Motivating Teachers

Addressing the needs of others is an important focus, but it is also important to develop yourself. Teachers need motivation too. Teacher training is an ongoing process. Romans 2:19–21 asks us why we don't teach ourselves. If you are indeed sure that you are someone else's guide, why not position yourself to be fed? Attend Bible studies offered in your church where you are not the teacher. Regularly attend conferences, workshops, or seminars in your region. You can feed from the fellowship of persons in another context who do what you do and experience similar realities. There are conferences for leaders you can attend and literature you could read on spiritual leadership. Request your pastor to provide information regarding opportunities for growth. As a leader, develop relationships with leaders in other churches. Pool your resources for a broader scope.

Why wouldn't the local church routinely hold such events and encourage attendance in other places by sponsoring its members? The church should give financial support when possible. In all professions, the employer provides some form of professional development or training. Why shouldn't the church be the sponsor of opportunities for willing workers to grow?

The minister or director of Christian education or the Sunday school superintendent should keep a record of those who participate and find out why others do not participate. Use their responses to restructure what is being done in the workers meetings so that their needs are met. It does not benefit the Lord for countless hours of planning to be spent if the needs of the teachers are not met. Develop a user-friendly technique with the staff just as each staff member creates a nurturing atmosphere for his or her class. Soon afterward, hold them accountable. Where there is no accountability, there is often apathy. A church with teachers who are indifferent, lethargic, and lazy generally experience classes with boring lessons and poor attendance. Inconsistency and irregularity are other by-products with little to no accountability. Who is motivating whom? None of this is pleasing to God.

Teachers' needs must be met. Seminars or workshops for teachers should be designed to meet specific areas of concern. The desires of the leader should be rooted in providing support for the staff based on Christian principles. Vainglory has no place here; there is little fruit harvested in a field that is not cultivated. Focus the agenda on what will assist those who attend rather than what makes your job easier. Spend the time addressing the persons present. Avoid conversation about who should have come but did not. You probably have persons in your church with the gifts and skills needed for this kind of event.

Provide a balance of topics to address what needs to be developed, using various modalities (learning styles) as expected in the classrooms. Modeling the behavior you expect is motivational for others. (While revising this paragraph, I just realized that I am making a gigantic assumption that most Christian churches have teachers' meetings routinely. However, the reality is that someone reading *Reach Me with SMILES* does not have gatherings of any sort for teachers in their church. If your church does not hold teachers' meetings, pray about beginning on a quarterly basis. I encourage you to speak with your pastor about the possibility and begin to affiliate with an association of churches in your region that can give you this kind of support.)

Training and Assessing Workers

Some method of evaluation should also be used for the teaching ministry of the church. Develop a forum to review a needs assessment. Then, take the time to make the most of the information or feedback received. Leaders need to keep their fingers on the pulse of the willing workers to keep them motivated as they continually seek to motivate their students. Picture the teacher as a team captain. The class represents the team. The captain is responsible for preparing the team or making (teaching) disciples. The teacher is a part of the team, a disciple who is developing other disciples. Because the disciples are effectively motivated, they become disciple makers themselves. The minister or director of Christian education serves as a coach. Coaches are responsible for preparing all the disciples, including themselves.

How do you assess disciple making? Look for the fruit. It is acceptable to God to hold people accountable for what they do in Jesus' name. John 15:8 says that you show yourselves to be disciples by how much fruit you bear. The successes of teachers can be shared during a time of testimony about the teaching-learning process at regular teachers' meetings. Here is an opportunity to be proactive. Role-play issues. However, be sure to focus *more* on the solution than the problem.

Do not be discouraged or disheartened by the number of persons in attendance at training sessions. Work effectively with those who are present. Some things addressed need to be handled in small groups. When something needs to be corrected, address it rather than let it linger. Agree concerning what they ask. It will be done for them by God because two or three are gathered together in Jesus' name. (Matthew 18:15–20). Don't be overly concerned about low attendance. Take full advantage of it. If you really want more to come, literally feed them at least once a quarter. We do like to eat together. Not every meeting has to have a rigid agenda.

On the other hand, if your numbers are fifteen or more, some of the sessions could be broken down into small groups of two to three for more sharing time from each participant. Then, come back as a whole group for closing comments. Teachers whose classes have the same age ranges can be grouped together for one approach but separated for another. Decide that according to what you are trying to achieve. If you want a weaker teacher to hear how a stronger teacher handles a particular part of a lesson, design the grouping that would put them together. Who is best at doing what? Considerations include but are not limited to age groups, use of technology, using other visuals, planning, writing a lesson outline, getting students involved, etc. Give them opportunity to share during the meetings. Attendance may grow when value increases; give them what they say they need. Model approaches to teaching by using them as formats for the meetings.

Dynamic lessons take time to plan and meetings could highlight techniques for the lessons as well as the exegesis (interpretation, clarification, definition, and word studies) of the text. Take the time to read various things on the topic or issue before class so that there is a fresh perspective to share. Some of the lessons that we think are interesting and exciting are boring. They may have been developed with the needs or experiences of the teacher as the driving force. They may have been used before but are not relevant to the current group. Or the teacher may have been a lazy, last-minute preparer. It is difficult to motivate someone to do something that you are not willing to do yourself.

Help me to study the Word to show myself approved by Jesus.

If your church has not had regular teachers' meetings or it has been a few years since you have had them, the following ideas may help you stoke the fire.

Training Session Suggestion 1
(60–90 minutes)

Prayer and praise

10 minutes Questionnaire/Survey

Take the time to design questions that you really want to have answered.

15 minutes Introductions—One minute or less each

Attendees share something in particular that others may not know about them, such as place of birth, hobby, or collector of something.

15 minutes Topic: What the Scripture Says about Teaching/Training

15 minutes Topic: Where Do We Go from Here?

Record responses so they can verify it is what they said (flipchart, poster-size Post-It paper, etc.). Use it later for further staff development.

5 minutes Prayer and dismissal

Training Session Suggestion 2
(60–90 minutes)

Prayer and praise

15 minutes Topic: Problem/Solution

Role-Play Issues—Be sure to focus *more* on the solutions than problems

30 minutes Topic: Prioritizing and Implementing

Where must *I* start?

- Develop a strategy or a function of the specific groups of persons according to what they do— teachers of certain age groups, class secretaries, fellowship leaders, prayer leaders, etc.

- Agree upon a time/place for monthly or quarterly sharing—brainstorming, pooling of resources, combined training with other churches, networking (leaders, departments, teachers, secretaries, etc.).

15 minutes Topic: Look at the Literature

Read something ahead of time so that there is always a fresh perspective to share at the gatherings.

15 minutes Evaluation, prayer, and dismissal

Suggestions for Other Sessions

A. Meeting Purpose: Prayer

Meet together for an hour of prayer.

Each person participates.

Read a passage from the Bible.

Lift concerns of the teaching ministry separately: workers, students, leaders.

Have nothing but prayer for the gathering.

B. Meeting Purpose: Fellowship

Bonding or specific celebration

Affirm one another

No agenda

Practice

Use the following passages to help you remember why you are a Christian educator.

John 14:1–13   Jesus has prepared a place for us.

John 14:14–19   Jesus will not leave us as orphans.

John 16:13–14   The Spirit guides you into *all* the truth.

Acts 2   The Holy Spirit came.

Romans 1:1–7   Bondservant of Christ.

Romans 8:16, 28   Does your spirit line up?

2 Timothy 1:5–9   Are you sincere?

Point to Ponder

Meditate on this verse: Ephesians 3:20, 21.

Write any thoughts that come to your mind, and then describe your feelings.

Summary

- Training teachers is an ongoing process.

- Conferences, workshops, or seminars should be held routinely and attendance at such events sponsored outside of your church should be encouraged. Financial support should be given by the church when possible.

- Addressing the needs of others is as important as developing self.

- Initiate and restructure workers' meetings to meet specific needs.

- Evaluate and self-assess continually to motivate believers, teachers, and learners.

- Be proactive by taking advantage of effective training.

Involve

Reach out to me.
Involve me. Include me. Keep me coming to Bible classes regularly.

Involve

How do you teach a Bible lesson that will assist believers with spiritual growth? Reach them with involvement. Give them opportunities to share, to participate, or to implement their ideas with various teaching techniques. Allow believers to take part in choosing the activity. Occasionally letting students tell you what they want to do keeps you fresh and free from burnout. A wealth of information and ideas can be found when you take the time to look for it. It could be right before your very eyes.

Teaching to Transform

We have always done some things effectively in our teaching for some time now. How long have you taught in the church? Think of how society has changed within that time. Did the context of our teaching ministry change? Does your style reflect the way you were taught or the way you taught when you started years ago? Now may be the time that a transformation takes place within your mind so that the master teacher measures your teaching strategies.

Transformation implies that a change is in order. What does the change involve? There is a literal change in form. The structure that has been used is modified but not totally discarded. Transformed teaching is the result of the teachers cutting across their standard procedures and making different connections with the students and the Word of God. Therefore, the change is personal. The teacher develops the desire to be different, to teach differently, and to use different approaches.

When we are transformed, our methods have need of change. If we are different from the way we were, then there is internal friction or discomfort. Your teaching style and your new lifestyle are not in alignment. Likewise, your students are being asked to grow in the Lord and you look for the evidence of that spiritual growth. Do the people who attend church with us see growth in us? Has our lack of methodological transformation stunted personal growth and student growth? Could there be more student-centered teaching and involvement with Jesus as the model for both teacher and student? Just as students need to hear a Word from the Lord, the Christian educator does too. How often do you hear from God *while* teaching? The Holy Spirit can move in your preparation as well as during lesson delivery.

God wants his people to be delivered from the things that separate us from him. Being stuck in practices that no longer work can stunt the effects of teaching now. There are times when we should resort to tried-and-true methods. However, there are times when there is something better. What is the Lord saying *today* about how he wants the lesson on a familiar passage to be taught for today's believers? Sometimes, teachers who have been teaching for a while need a reconnection to the source and purpose of Christian teaching. The reconnection is a transformation. Rethink how you teach and why you teach, and transform your style. Modify approaches to accommodate the passage being taught. Let the Scripture and the Holy Spirit guide the method. We can attend workshops and find cute activities and approaches. We transport them to our context before considering whether they are appropriate to the scriptural text. There is a time and place for everything (Ecclesiastes 3:1–3), but keep it in the perspective of using the best method for the concept lifted for the specific scriptural lesson.

Are you a seasonal teacher? In years past, you were the king or queen of the overhead transparency. Next, you used the videocassette for everything. Before you knew it, you were overusing the computer with the LCD projector to PowerPoint pictures, outlines, notes, and anything else you could imagine. Do you pick up trends in teaching for the sake of the trend?

Currently technology is everywhere. I often use it in teaching; however, sometimes the mechanism distracts the message. Then, the nature of the student-centered lesson is lost. Use technology as it directly fosters the involvement of the learners. A PowerPoint presentation could be three slides and not thirty—just enough to arrest the attention, capture the image, provoke discussion, or delineate steps in a process. Every lesson is not the right season for the technology (or whatever trendy method is in vogue). Sometimes, I still show up with the Bible in my hand and nothing else. The method depends on what is needed to transfer the message, the issue, or concept of that lesson to specific students. We teach people.

Are you the kind of seasonal teacher who overuses trends at the cost of losing chances to seize teachable moments? **Teachable moments** seem to appear out of anything at any time. They are those times that you don't plan to delve into an illustration or point, but the opportunity is right there. You could not have planned it, but you could seize the moment because the lesson was well prepared. It is so easy just to describe the scene or event because it boomeranged where the students were mentally engaged at the time. There is a season of opportunity for every learner to be reached. Everyone is savable and everyone is teachable.

There are so many possible teaching seasons to consider for everyone involved. In season and out of season, always base the lesson on the Scripture. However, is it the season to build the students or chastise them? Is it a season for new faces or the same old faces week after week? Is it the season of a hot moral issue or social debate? For any age group, what season is it? How can you use the season to involve the students? Would you use the same type of fertilizer for houseplants, lawns, and crops? Surely, you recognize the need to diversify instruction to reach all who come. Is it time to change your kind of fertilizer? Your crop may be in need of a different formula because an immune deficiency occurred. You no longer see the effects you think you should see. Look at yourself before placing blame anywhere else. Maybe growth is stunted because appropriate "fertilizer" is lacking.

The student is in the growing season and the teacher is disconnected. The student is budding and the teacher is sitting in a disengaged state. The student is emerging and the teacher is detached. Perhaps the teacher does not recognize that she is somewhere else and needs to mentally relocate and transform some methods. Is the teacher trying to force the whole group to conform to a standard that is no longer standard? Has the teacher become dull of hearing? Does the teacher need someone to teach them again fundamental principles? (Hebrews 5:11–12).

How do you teach a Bible lesson that will assist believers with spiritual growth? Change your standard method from season to season. Allow students to be actively involved in their Christian education as a requirement in various stages of the teaching-learning process. Involve all learners regardless of age. Adults need variety as much as children or even more. Examine yourselves! (2 Corinthians 13:5, 6).

Jesus Christ is in you, and he is the model. Jesus did not use only one method to reach people to whom he ministered. He allowed their involvement in the process. He engaged them. When direct involvement in the teaching-learning process is a two-way street, more learning takes place. Transformative teaching is teaching that changes form or structure based on one standard: the Bible. Transformative teaching is teaching that has Jesus as the model for the believer, both teacher and student alike. Transformative teaching reaches people where they are and brings about deliverance, hence transfiguration.

Teaching for Transfiguration

Transfiguration is a type of reformation and is another type of restructuring. It is rethinking; it forms something again. A different framework results from a metamorphosis that occurs for the teacher and student as they share God's truths in holistic ways. Using these strategies should become part of a perpetual process. Using this method yields more effective, life-altering, transfigurative teaching; stimulate, motivate, and involve believers in the process of teaching and learning. How can this be implemented?

With the intention of reaching the people of God for their spiritual growth, the teacher must be receptive to spiritual food for personal growth. Transfiguration is personal. The first consideration is the teacher as the learner. After God has revealed himself *to you* through the Holy Spirit, he will work *through you* to reach others in the way that they need to be reached. Do you see the role of the teacher as tantamount to being a spiritual leader in the church? As a spiritual leader, you accept responsibility for the sheep in your pasture (class). Granted, the pastor is overseer of the whole flock. When you accept the responsibility of teaching in the church, you are agreeing to assist with the nurture of some of the sheep. As stated earlier in "Cultivating Deliberate Disciples," the pastor is still Jesus Christ's under shepherd; as a teaching ministry leader you are under the under shepherd. It is after you have sat with the Word and let it permeate your own heart (Romans 2:19–21) that you will have a heart to hear how to transmit the message of the lesson to someone else, but never in contradiction to the leadership of the pastorate.

Yes, teaching is an awesome responsibility. It is a gift of the Holy Spirit; the same Spirit empowers you and allows you to do what you do. Why not involve the sheep as often as possible and as much as possible? Their involvement becomes your barometer of effectiveness. Plan to take advantage of everything they offer to the teaching-learning process. More than one person will receive the message from the Scripture; therefore, use a variety of techniques and approaches for your lessons. No one method will work effectively all the time. Consider the key concept and context of the lesson and then meditate on how God wants you to deliver it for the understanding of others. How does a particular person in your group learn best? Modality is simply the method by which they perceive and understand.

Fashion the facts to fit the face of the learners for the lesson in front of you. That kind of interpretation facilitates application of the lesson. Less time will have to be spent in class reading the Scripture and more time on developing and applying the concepts. Believers are more likely to read before class because they know that they will be given an opportunity to make it fit their particular situations in life.

Consequently, the learner is the second-most important feature in lesson preparation. No, I am not overlooking the importance of the presence of God's truth; the content is the base on which the teacher and the student stand regardless of the dominant teaching-learning style. One person is verbal (a talker) but another person is more auditory (a listener). On the other hand, Sister Let-Me-See-It is visual (show me) while Brother Let-Me-Do-It is kinesthetic (let me touch it). It is not so important that the teacher have this or that style of teaching. The important thing becomes removing yourself so that others are reached for Christ by any means necessary and available.

How will the lesson provide for spiritual transfiguration? Consider the context of biblical transfiguration. Not everybody will be able to see it, but they will hear it and believe. Jesus told all of the disciples of his suffering, death, and coming glory. Six days later, he took three of them to the mount of transfiguration where they saw his face shine like the sun. They saw Moses and Elijah talking with Jesus. Not *all* of the disciples were able to see the transformation that revealed his future glory. Jesus told the three when it would be appropriate for the others to *hear* of it (Matthew 16:27–17:8; Mark 9:1–10).

Has anyone seen Jesus while you were teaching? Is it possible today? How will the lesson provide for the spiritual transfiguration of you and the believers?

Practice

Read these items with self-reflection. Pray for God to block out others so you can focus on yourself.

1. Read the text devotionally apart from reading it to study.
2. Observe what the Scripture says.
3. Interpret what it means to you.
4. Apply how it relates to your situation in life.
5. Later, list methods of presentation that capture the context and concept.
6. Reach the students! Teach them to read the passages of Scripture for themselves, observe what it says, interpret what it means, and apply how it relates to today.

7. Go to the session expecting that they will begin to read at home daily during the week and show them by example how that enriches your life.

8. After the lesson has been taught, take the time to evaluate it.

    a. How did the lesson provide for spiritual transfiguration?

    b. What is the **effect** of using your gift of teaching?

    c. How does your gift **affect** your relationships?

Jesus did not approach his life and ministry haphazardly. His mission was far too important. He gave his best; He gave his all. His approach and method were appropriate for the time, setting, and people to whom he related. As a result, people characterized his teaching as new, authoritative, and different from the teaching they heard from others. In John 13:12–15, Jesus told them to do as he had done. Jesus modeled his message and used a variety of approaches. He used parables (stories), objects, drama, discussions, questions and answers, and lectures. He was innovative; he taught anytime, anywhere, with resources on hand. Teaching with Jesus as the model means teaching a message clearly for spiritual transformation[2] and transfiguration.

To summarize, transfigurative teaching is sort of like structural renovation. The structure of your lesson outline is changed to a different view. Embracing a framework that is unusual for you results from a metamorphosis—a change for the teacher and student from the inside outward.

Points to Ponder

Spend a period of meditation considering **transformation** and **transfiguration** in the Bible.

1. What is the point surrounding each of these two verses? Consider the verses that precede and follow each.

   a. Romans 12:2

   b. 2 Corinthians 3:18

2. What does each of the passages have in common?

   a. Matthew 17:2–13

   b. Mark 9:2–13

   c. Luke 9:28–36

3. How is each of the passages different?

4. How can the similarities and differences be applied to teaching today?

5. How is John 1:14 similar to the three passages above?

6. Distinguish transformation and transfiguration.

Setting Goals and Objectives

Specific goals and objectives must be measurable; you can determine that they have been accomplished. Objectives are statements that describe the specific action that is desired as the result of a specific lesson. The objective then is something that can be observed by others; it can be seen and not just heard. The objective defines a specific action that demonstrates that the goal has been achieved. Goals are broader biblical concepts that emerge from the lessons that are to be applied to the life of the believer. The teacher and the student should be able to determine whether the goals and objectives are being met. For example, the believer is able to forgive a relative for something that happened years ago. The believer shows mercy after participating in a lesson from Matthew 5:7, 23:23 and/or Romans 5:8.

Develop a guiding purpose statement for the lesson that is based directly on the Scripture at hand. Glean the statement from a passage or a single verse. Design everything in the lesson that day to uplift the concept in the statement. It will guide all activities and the development of questions toward a particular purpose. Justice, mercy, and faith are weightier matters of the law, but the lesson's focus is mercy. A comparison or contrast can be made among them, but the emphasis is to develop one of the three: mercy.

Because of a more thorough investigation of mercy, the believer may choose to alter something about his life that reflects the choice to change. That is a measurable behavior. What can a person do to show mercy? Not only *say* you forgive because of the conviction from being justified by faith but also *treat* the individual differently. The believer will be able to show forgiveness is a measurable objective under the broader goal to discuss various aspects of mercy.

Setting specific goals and objectives helps keep the Christian educator focused on the purpose of Christian teaching. Jesus Christ is the source of Christian teaching. Christian teachers teach to develop lives for Christ; the ultimate goal of reconciliation and relationship with God must be embedded in each lesson. Therefore, the Christian educator must move from nonevangelistic lesson outlines toward a "new people coming in" mentality. Each lesson must reach others for Jesus today. The believers will walk out with the Word this week and will be compelled to share it with others. The activities selected for the lesson reflect the complexity of learning styles of the persons present and consequently involve most of them. When the purpose of the teaching moment is clear to the teacher and procedures are implemented that focus on the one objective, results can be measured.

Believers will share testimonies of experiences with God or personal evangelism. Because of a specific act of forgiveness, not only does God bless the one who forgave but also the person being forgiven. The persons who observe the dynamics of the revitalized relationship are affected as well. Lifestyle changes will be evident as seen in demeanor, conversation, and ministry involvement when testimonies are shared. Set up a class atmosphere that intentionally facilitates sharing, which will be a method of measuring the goals and objectives.

To facilitate improved teacher performance, we must **prepare ourselves** in the Word by doing the same three things we want the lesson to bring out of the believers: **observe** what it says, **interpret** what it says, and **apply** what it says. Then we can set a goal based on the reading. Read the Scripture in different versions to observe what the message is from the Holy Spirit. Use the version that is easiest for you to understand for general reading and rereading (King James, New King James, New American Standard, New International, Good News, etc.). Read it to feel it. Later as you study, you observe every word and how each word is placed in each sentence in a certain order. Observe how the verse would be different if a particular word was not there. Though you read different versions and different words, one goal of the verse will become apparent for your edification and later for your teaching. Then, write down the nuances within a version or different changes you have observed as you compare other versions.

Interpret what it says and apply what it says to your own life and experiences before planning to teach. As you study the Bible, make sure that you take the time to *observe* the context then *interpret* what the Word says. Do not be too quick to jump to *application* because you may have missed a nuance that is the life-altering hinge.

Improving personal performance prepares you to involve students more effectively. Perhaps you have not read anything in this process that is a new thought for you. That's great! This gives opportunity to unclutter something that lies within you. Retrace your steps. Possibly, you have piled on so much over the years that you have forgotten who you are and why you teach. Getting rid of the clutter releases you to recognize a kind of self-separation, dividing one part of who you are from another. You can begin to reprioritize those parts. As your journey of rediscovery continues, you approach application for teaching once more. What are you supposed to do as a disciple, trainer, or nurturer, and how do you get it done? Discipleship, discipleship training, and nurturing are all processes, too. Where are you as a disciple? Never lose sight of that.

There has to be a goal or an intentional purpose for what you do as a teacher that points others toward Christ. A goal is something that you want to achieve that can be measured. Stop and think for a moment about a lesson that impacted you. There was a specific aim that targeted you as a believer in order for the teacher's mission or objective for the day to be accomplished. (I am assuming that you not only teach but also make it a priority to be taught.) What was the objective or goal of that lesson? You might say understanding the Word or learning to depend on God more.

Now think about what you will be teaching next. Let's ask the same question differently. What are the achievements that you anticipate because of teaching this lesson? How many ways can you say the same thing as you reinforce that one message? Now the answers may be communicating with God, listening to his Word, obedience, positive attitudes, etc. As a result of teaching these specific lessons, what achievements do you anticipate? How will you know that believers have achieved the goal, or how do you measure what believers achieve? How do you know that someone learned obedience? You might say that believers could apply it to their daily lives through their testimony, walk, or actions. It is good for a believer to know the broad or general goals of bringing others to Christ and meeting Jesus face-to-face one day. It is also necessary to know in the meantime, or as I tarry day-by-day, "What will I do with myself? *Today*, I need to work on being obedient."

How does a teacher get this point across? Answers to that question come when you are studying. Specifically, how does one work on being obedient? The answer should be located in that Scripture lesson, unless you pulled something that was not in that particular passage and you need to reread it. Coming up with the "obedience" and "listening to God" is what you receive in your spirit as a teacher while you are reading for personal edification. Remember that reading and studying are two different steps: yourself in relation to the Lord (what the Bible says and what the Holy Spirit tells you about you at the time you read it) then yourself in relation to other people. Always know that Jesus holds things together.

If your Bible teaching is for a particular purpose, ask the question that will lead you to where you are trying to go. Use as many methods or activities as time will allow, repeating the same objective to ensure that the main point is made. Some people are more gifted with the ability to think on their feet and ask poignant questions while others need to exert more effort and energy. One is not better than the other is; each is equally effective. Most things can be taught if a person is willing to learn. If you need more practice with asking the right questions to achieve the desired effect, consider the stem of the question. Look at the first few words of a question. For basic facts, use the type of question that requires lower-level thinking. Who? What? Where? When? These help you to get started. However, do not load your lesson with these because they are prone to keeping the believers at a lower level of spiritual maturity. You want to grow people. Deal with issues. Move toward asking open-ended questions where any answer is acceptable. These questions may include the following:

"In your opinion …"

"What you would do if …?"

"Have you ever been faced with …?"

"Has there been a time when …?"

"Would you like to share a time when …?"

"What did the verse say to you …?"

"How does it speak to your life …?"

Teachers need to understand the process of learning to be a disciple or follower of Jesus. In addition, teachers need to understand discipleship training as a process to recognize which stage they are working on at a particular time with each individual. Therefore, we would be in a better position to know on which part of the process a particular lesson should focus. The Holy Spirit provides this wisdom; we need to know to ask for it as we prepare. Our students need to know that we care about them enough to systematically plan toward specific goals and objectives if we are going to be effective. Believers may not want to sit in a class with someone who is not willing to show himself and share experiences as the Holy Spirit relates all of it to the Scripture at hand. Teachers become facilitators of a faith walk with Jesus. Become the expert of the *process* of learning about the Lord and share the benefits to bless those who sojourn as co-laborers in Christ.

General goals, objectives, and specific achievements are at work here. How do you write the exact achievement that believers will be able to demonstrate as a direct result of participating in this lesson? If they get only get one point, what is that point, Lord? Be very intentional about writing down a statement that represents the one thing that believers will take with them as a result of the next lesson that you teach. Take a moment and ponder that point now.

Always take a moment for reflection in your reading, study, and preparation for teaching. If you need to process your thoughts as you prepare, believers probably need to process as they receive messages in a learning environment that is conducive for the Holy Spirit to move. Slow down, sometimes, for a few seconds of reflection. Respect quiet, think time, even in the classroom.

Improving Preparation Techniques

- **Set a teaching objective or goal** based on your personal time with the Word. If you were teaching, what would be the goal? Process the concept of the verse. Identify the concept in order to write a single statement.

- **Isolate key words** in order to help you focus on a teaching point or specific goal. Does each version use the same key words? Choose the words that would be inoffensive to persons in your group rather than trigger words that produce negative images. For example, some versions use *master* as opposed to *teacher*. Depending on the depth of a person's ethnicity, an issue of authority may come up in a person's mind that takes them in different direction. You do not perceive it until they ask something or make a statement that leaves you wondering, *How did they get that out of what I said?* Lead with *teacher* and later substitute *master* as you go and the word *master* is understood as *teacher*; you intentionally take people from where they are to where you want them to go. (The assumption here is that you continually take the time to build relationships and that you know the people that comprise your class. Even when there is a new individual or visitor present, there is a built-in time of sharing that makes everyone comfortable and gives you an opportunity to begin to know him or her from the beginning of the class session.)

- Discern words that may cause trouble because you are person minded. Make sure that your terminology helps you to connect to where believers are. Do not avoid issues; simply be aware of how you address them.

- Choose words that are authentic for you not outside of your personality. Don't be too colloquial if that's not you. Do not intentionally use words that are outside of who you are in an effort to reach others, especially youth. Keep it real because people know when you are not and you may be perceived as phony.

- **Distinguish teaching points from broader concepts**. Stay focused under the leadership of the Holy Spirit rather than diverging to every specific detail at an inappropriate moment.

- **Consider the context**. For example, we cannot deal with John 13:13 in isolation; we must go back at least to John 13:1–12. Also under consideration must be chapters 1–12 and whether or not there is a chapter 14; what does it say in connection to the others? Then, you might be in a position to share the fruit of your study with somebody else.

- **Come up with questions against the Scripture.** Challenge the Scripture by asking it questions. Use terminology to be people friendly but not out of your character. Move the people from where they are to where you want them to go as a result of what you know you are trying to achieve: the concept, goal, objective.

- Effective teaching depends on your ability to make it relevant and keep it real. By the time people walk out of the teaching session, what is it that you really want them to have in their heart? Jesus is Lord and teacher.

- Asking questions does not necessarily mean that people are going to walk out with the answer that leads to the concept of the day. Keep focused on the one point that they will leave with. Regardless of the length or liveliness of discussions that may arise during the course of the session, what do they need to know?

- Raise a question that will be relevant to the everyday life of your group. It does not need to be a factual question. Come up with something that believers need to wrestle with at least a little bit so that it can penetrate deep within their spirit. Who was the master teacher? Was Jesus the master teacher? Believers may silently beg you to feed them more than the obvious. How is the Lord the teacher in your life? Why do I need Jesus to teach me anything? To what extent is Jesus the master in your life? Why is Jesus considered the greatest teacher?

- Phrase the question in a way that the listener clearly understands what is being asked. If the question is too long, the hearer may not know your intent. You may need to break the longer thoughts into smaller pieces, chunks that assist you in leading to the ultimate question. Put the thought into a capsule so that you are sure to get to where you want to go.

- Now, identify the one statement for the Scripture you are about to teach. The statement of purpose should not be too long. Eventually, you will be coming up with activities to support it; hence, brevity keeps the teacher as preparer focused.

- Too many important concepts within one purpose statement make the process of choosing activities confusing and possibly frustrating due to time constraints.

- Build a brief sentence from which other statements, questions, or activities can be developed. The person may clearly understand what the teacher said ought to be true from the Christian's perspective. For example, "I understand the teacher said I should acknowledge Jesus as my teacher." Whether believers confess within their hearts that Jesus is their teacher is another matter. The concept has to be clearly taught before the student can walk out with a message for God to increase within them.

Points to Ponder

- Know yourself.
- Intentionally establish positive relationships with the people that you lead (your class) on a continuing basis. How are we going to teach people if we do not take time to get to know them?
- Share yourself. How do you include what you like to do in your ministry of teaching for Christ without continual lecture and soapbox?

- Apply what you receive from the Word. How does that biblical message connect to my life? Then explore, "How can I teach it?"

- Effective goals and objectives must be measurable. What are the achievements that you anticipate because of teaching this lesson?

- Don't give an overload of information. Keep it simple, saints (a holy KISS).

- One important thing in this process is knowing where you are trying to go and using appropriate terminology to get you there without losing anybody. When you sense that someone is not where you are in thought for whatever the reason, the teacher is responsible for pausing to make sure things are cleared up. It may be a facial expression or other body language. Keep them involved.

- Be aware of making assumptions as you lead discussions. One could assume that they are considering the Lord as their teacher. You saying it does not make it so. People make choices daily, and we need to acknowledge free will daily.

- When teaching, be sure to give them some think time to ponder the question. Let the room be silent before rushing to call on someone or to give a personal discourse. The questions should connect to the people in the class rather than to the teacher per se. Does the "you" in your questioning force them to look at themselves or their teacher? You want the Word to penetrate their hearts. Be careful that the attention is pointing away from the teacher as the center; the connection is to be made that relates to the individuals present so that they can walk out with it, use it, and share that message with others for Christ.

- Remember that the passages we read in the Bible had one original meaning with multiple applications. You can more effectively teach one at a time. Reading the Bible daily and studying it are two different things; effective teachers do both. Read every word in context, recognizing that the use of a word changes over the centuries. In addition, you must follow a process as you spiritually prepare yourself then prepare to teach. You must observe, interpret, and apply the scriptural text. The more you apply this process and the more you teach, the more you should grow and be able to help others grow in the Lord.

Practice

Repeat the process again. Remember the importance of repetition, as you want the believers to mimic biblical lessons in their lives to bring them closer to Christ. Observe, interpret, and apply Ezekiel 36:26–28.

Summary

You are sitting at home reading the Bible. Then you are studying the Bible. Now, pretend that the class is in session and you are concluding the lesson. The purpose statement is like jumping so far ahead in lesson preparation that you are at the end of the process. So we ask, "What is the point of this passage?" Once you know what you have received from the Holy Spirit from meditating with different versions of the same passage, you have the point or the concept. At this time, you are ready to consider methods, procedures, and other questions that can be used to fill in the remainder of the lesson. Spend the most time in lesson preparation absorbing the Word in a personal way. Do you know who you are? Are you meditating on the Word personally? Is your preparation for teaching being guided by what you think you are going to get out of the process of teaching? "What is the point?"

The controlling factor after your spirit has been fed needs to be feeding God's sheep. The brief purpose statement along with a lesson title can control your thinking. As you focus on the specific message that will feed someone, acknowledge the place of the Holy Spirit. Ultimately, he or she may be drawn closer to the Lord. The teacher spiritually transforms so that he or she facilitates the believer's transfiguration. Lifestyles change as the teacher and student draw closer to God.

For Further Reading

Johnston, Jay and Ronald Brown. *Teaching the Jesus Way: Building a Transformational Teaching Ministry.* Nashville: LifeWay Press, 2000.

Love

Reach out to me.
Love me by modeling the Lord. Discipline me so that I am able to
practice what I am learning by seeing it in seasoned saints.

Love

How do you teach a Bible lesson that will assist believers with spiritual growth? The Christian educator should stimulate, motivate, involve, and love each of the sheep entrusted to them. We have expounded upon a variety of approaches to reach students; we now turn to a very basic tenet of the Christian faith. Reach learners with love. Once the atmosphere is set for stimulating discoveries of the Word, individuals are compelled to participate, and you are so personally prepared that their involvement is evident. Do not neglect the basic demonstrations of loving them. Love is what love does; let your actions show your love.

You might ask, "How many ways can I show or tell my students that I love them?" Show love according to John 15:12–14 and show that you are a friend of the Lord. How does Jesus' love feel to you? How does it feel to be Jesus' friend? We must develop relationships with them, overtly demonstrating that we love the people before us. You have to feel that you love them. You must know that you do.

Many times in Deuteronomy, the people of God were admonished to love him. The love was shown through specific acts of sacrifice, offering, resisting idol worship, and being in good relationship with one another. The commandment that Jesus gives us does not give us a choice if we want to be his friend. We must love one another.

How should you show yourself friendly in a teaching-learning environment? The same way you do anywhere else. It becomes a part of your personality as a Christian. Though you compartmentalize yourself when studying the Word of God to determine what facet of your character God is addressing at the time, you are still only one person. Your personality is either loving or it's not. Be aware of yourself, what you do or say turns people on or off. How does your personality show love? How can you generate an authentic loving atmosphere? What do you do to make the students *feel* Jesus the way you do when you know that he loves you? Pursue love (1 Corinthians 14:1). Be intentional about following after love.

Demonstrating Love

Roman Christians showed their love for Paul by being present for him. The sacrifice was made to go the distance, literally, to get to him (Acts 28:15). The King James Version uses the word *charity* in 1 Corinthians 13:1 to explain what love might look like. Charity is described as the greatest of the three Christian graces: faith, hope, and charity (1 Corinthians 12:31–13:13).

Love is more than a display of intellect, which was worshiped in the days of Paul. When your teaching becomes mostly "heady," love reconnects the learner to the lesson. Do not resound like brass. Your ability to understand deep mysteries or your abiding faith and knowledge about the Word of God are nothing if the participants do not sense that you love them. Show your love by what you give to them with patience and kindness. Avoid the appearance of being boastful, envious, rude, or seeking your own glory. Be aware of how you react to things your students say. Do not show that you are annoyed or angry about their contributions to the class. Show that you value them, what they say, and what they do. That is what love looks like.

Christian educators fulfill part of the Great Commission—making disciples. We are doing "whatsoever" Jesus commanded. Believers who come to us are saying, "Reach me by loving me." After self-reflection, you might be spiritually ready to lead others lovingly to a closer relationship with Christ. That's the heart of Christian discipline.

I have conducted many workshops, seminars, and retreats where the question came up about discipline in a church classroom. Colossians 3:12–17 speaks of what we should do. Since we are the elect of God, we should put on what looks like God. We must bear with one another and forgive one another. Christ forgives us! If we will let the peace of God rule in our hearts, the product is love, even when believers are not behaving in a manner that we agree with at a particular time. When the word of Christ lives in you, Christian classroom discipline is not impossible, teaching and admonishing one another in love.

Applying Discipline in Love

Why should we discuss discipline in this context? All learners need to know that you care enough to invest the time it takes to understand them. We need to give attention to this in our churches as we train our teachers. How does one teach a Bible lesson that enhances spiritual transfiguration? Love me by leading me. Lead me by teaching me how to apply the Word of God to every aspect of my life. Lead me by loving me with accountability for my actions, comments, and thoughts. Sometimes, problems handling discipline stem from personal perceptions, self-confidence, or relationships. As you continue to read, understand that discipline applies to any age group—children, youth, young adults, and older adults alike.

What is discipline? We can mean different things when we say discipline, and people who hear us may be thinking something totally different. For example, *Merriam-Webster's Collegiate Dictionary* gives these among other definitions of discipline: a field of study; training that corrects, molds, or perfects; punishment; control gained by obedience or training; orderly conduct; a system of rules governing conduct. There is a set of verbs that describe the actions of people who discipline: punish, train, or develop, bring under control, impose order. Which of these do you mean when you speak of discipline?

From my studies in college to become a special education teacher years ago, it was taught that discipline could be negative or positive. Negative discipline generally renders some form of punishment for undesirable behavior. Goals are set and a program or plan of action is developed of activities that lead toward that goal. Positive discipline, on the other hand, refers to a planned series of activities or exercises considered necessary for the attainment of a certain goal. This positive training would include routine activities with things that are allowed and other things that are restricted.

Generally, this describes the way we function on any job without a lot of complaint because we sense the need for some structure. In school, a curriculum leads to a certificate, a diploma, or a degree. For an athlete, intensive training can lead to winning. A mechanic's apprenticeship may lead to someday managing or owning a shop. Commonly, a set of rules must be adhered to for adequate positive discipline to be maintained. What would the community be without guidelines for practicing law or medicine? The implication for the Christian educator is that there are guidelines the church must follow and they are found in the Bible. A practicing Christian must exercise positive discipline in fear of God, who will punish or reward when eternity comes.

Another way of viewing discipline is with the thought that one person or authority limits the behavior of another. If the person in authority is not imposing the boundaries, the spectator may think, *They need discipline.* Perhaps what they observed was part of the carefully prepared lesson structured as a lively rather than quiet activity. It is evident that there are different perspectives regarding what discipline is and what should be done about it. Regardless of which definition you use for a particular situation, there are implications for strategies that may be helpful to handle discipline effectively and lovingly in a Christian classroom. If a Christian is the teacher, I will call it a Christian classroom. I have used these ideas in different forums: schools for public, private, or incarcerated students as well as in church meetings.

There are as many discipline styles as there are perspectives on discipline. Punishment is most prevalent as a style to change undesirable behavior. Suppose God punished me for every indiscretion. Woe is me! If the teacher dictates discipline, it is centered on giving the teacher an expected outcome. That outcome is usually based on the teacher's perception of the behavior and the action toward changing it. Task-imposed discipline is limited to what is needed for that particular activity or event.

The group commands another style of discipline; the majority of the persons involved as a whole participate in the discipline process. Although there may be a place for each of these, self-imposed discipline is the goal toward which the Christian educator should strive. The *disciplinee* ultimately learns the biblical basis for godly character and an inward change manifests itself outwardly that others know that Jesus is in the heart. The teacher and the group are observers of each other, all learning and growing through the grace of God. That mission is possible. It is a process that will take time, but it is attainable with patience.

Another sobering thought on the matter is simply that not everybody who attends your class will choose to follow the precepts of God. Some will believe, some will doubt, and some will not believe. It is not up to the teacher to determine who fits each category. We must show the love of Jesus to all the same way.

There are also many **methods and techniques** of discipline. Arrange the learning environment to avoid difficulties and undesirable situations. This means that the teachers who plan only one day in advance have to change (transform) the way they prepare to teach. Time must be spent in prayerful meditation so that the Holy Spirit can deliver the plan of action to you. Only the Lord knows what the disciplinee is going to do. Seek first to hear from the Father through the Son so that the Spirit can advise you. That may not happen if you can only squeeze in a few hours the day before or the same morning you enter the learning arena. You would not be entering as the champion or the victor because you have set yourself up with the uncertainty of an incomplete plan for the people of God. The need for proper planning is affected by neither the age of believers nor the fact that they are male, female, or mixed groups. Disciplinary problems may be curtailed by more effective planning with the aid of the Holy Spirit. The loving Christian educator views problems as opportunities for God to use her to begin creating something new.

When problems or challenges arise that you would categorize under the umbrella of discipline, restructure the learning environment in some way; it does not have to be drastic. Stay focused on the message of the day. A soft glance can acknowledge the situation without a word spoken about the negativity. The words that follow the glance are the same words you were going to say. Or ask an open-ended question already planted in the lesson to redirect attention to the Word of God. Everyone present will know that you are aware of the disruption, but you chose the lesson as more important at that moment. The commotion can be addressed personally and privately later. The Holy Spirit has given you the direction for the lesson. (Your pastor or minister/director of Christian education may have assisted.) The enemy wants to take the focus away from God. That is not acceptable. Christian educators could view the role as a disturbance or confusion reducer. God is not the author of confusion.

This implies that we must particularly plan for circumstances that would thwart the delivery of the message of the day. If you know that a disciplinee often talks out of turn, use it to the benefit of the lesson. Plan questions or at least one activity that intentionally draws that person into discussion designed by the Scripture you are teaching. Let that person assist you in implementing the activity. Let him/her lead at least one of several small groups to answer a probing question. This way, more people have an opportunity to share, rather than having one person monopolize the center stage. Have the groups, or peer pairs, come back together and the spokespersons from each group present their conclusions. The participants are required to demonstrate love through mutual respect as each delivers his/her contribution.

Let God help you to set the stage. Create opportunities for them to experience God with minimal anxiety each time that they come into your learning environment. Making enough time for proper planning is a key factor. When distressing situations do arise, the question becomes "Holy Spirit, how do you want me to redirect their attention to God?" When you have planned well, you are not the anxiety producer; you have confidence in what you have been given to present. You also have confidence that the Spirit of God will indeed give you the words and the behavior for that very moment.

Your response could be simple body language. Slowly move close to the individual as you continue the procedures during discussion. They know what they are doing is annoying (or downright aggravating), and proximity calms them. Perhaps they just wanted attention. Give them positive attention. All that is needed, in some instances, is a physical change in where you position yourself in the room accompanied with a gentle smile, no words to address them. Continue the lesson or agenda. Do you believe in the God you teach? Teach and lead meetings like you believe so that believers experience how you summon the assistance of the Holy One. Nonbelievers who are present may experience the movement of the Holy Spirit and not even know what hit them. Hopefully, it wasn't you.

Appeal to the conscience of the disciplinee. A nod, laying a hand on the shoulder, or any other gesture that does not interfere with the learning environment may be all that is needed. Be aware of their body language as well, not encroaching their personal space if uninvited. If you make an emotional response that sounds or feels like a verbal assault, impatience, or a desire to be anywhere but near that person, your witness to them and the other students is weakened. Moreover, those most damaged may be the observers as opposed to the disciplinee.

If we equate discipline with maturity, we will see some similarities. People who are immature do not necessarily consider the result or the consequences of their actions beforehand or afterward. They form the perspective of what they want and where they currently exist. In contrast, a spiritually mature person's conscience would be pricked to know that something that they did or said caused an adverse reaction to someone else. As Christian educators, we must attempt to move a person from not caring what others think to caring that the environment was negatively affected because of something they said or did. Again, this does not refer to any specific age group; any group of people in any society has persons with different levels of social and spiritual maturity. That is not the problem. It is a challenge and another opportunity for God to be seen.

Another method or discipline technique would give the disciplinee less attention for undesirable behavior than may have been given previously. Sometimes, they are starving for attention and have used negative behaviors to get any attention they can. In order to get the attention they desire, require a disciplinee to exhibit desirable behaviors. We cannot afford to handle discipline in the same manner that may have created the undesirable behavior in the first place. We are Jesus' agents for changing hearts rather than making aggressors more aggressive. The Christian educator is Christ's emissary or ambassador.

If your disciplinary concern is that they won't let the teacher teach, consider that you may be talking too much. Or, you may be expecting the focus to be on you while someone is reflecting on a message God just delivered to them through you. Perhaps they refused to do something simple you asked. Are they acting out negatively because of something that hit them in the lesson? I remember a child who once told me she wanted another verse; she did not want to share from the one given. When I re-read it and looked in her face, I saw God moving her through a behavior that needed changing. She saw herself in the verse and acted out negatively, rejecting the need for a personal change. She ended up doing a great job interpreting that verse in front of the larger body of all the classes. She continues to show improved behavior in other ways as well.

What is teaching to you? From the previous sections, we find that teaching is more than one person speaking prepared information to a quiet, attentive group of listeners. Sometimes, they are listeners, but there are other aspects as well.

Add a few more open-ended questions to stir up the curiosity of the group. Use questions or statements that will cause them to question each other, then give them the opportunity to be engaged in the topic (minus your voice) for a few minutes. The ultimate goal of your teaching is to provide opportunities for believers to experience God in order to make life-altering decisions. A more Christlike change in lifestyle can stem from participation in discussions or short activities that are not contingent upon the teacher. Changing your role from *teacher* to *facilitator,* from time to time, enables changes to take place in your students' behavior. Their involvement in the lessons produces lasting impressions that can be replicated when they face life's challenges, long after leaving the session. Isn't that what we want? In order to get a handle on this discipline issue, we may first need to get a handle on ourselves: the way we prepare for a lesson and the signals we portray as we deliver it. *Be a tension reducer, not a stress inducer.* Do not provoke. Do not nag.

How can Christian educators teach and impose discipline? The people who come to our churches (including us) are the same people who make up society. Therefore, implications can be taken from that context. Since God has made information available to us, effectively use it to glorify the kingdom of God. If some Christian educators feel that they cannot be effective because one or two of believers are not "disciplined," what are they to do? One approach is to look at what discipline is and then see what Scripture has to say about it. None of this will mean anything without applying it to the contemporary situation that raised the initial question. How do Christian educators teach and impose discipline?

The idea here is to look at the implications that arrive from society as a whole, "society" loosely meaning gathered groups of people. Once we perceive the context of the persons exhibiting the undesired behavior, we have a better understanding of who they are. When saying undesired, I am referring to behavior that contradicts the Word of God; we are not talking about our own standards. We must back up everything we say, think, and do with the Bible. Christian educators teach discipline by going back to the Bible to find out how Jesus Christ taught it, then by taking believers to the Bible to show them where the Bible speaks of specifics for their situation. This requires that the teacher have a personal relationship with Christ and a sense of self-disciplined study with an active prayer life. From these come love, peace, and patience (longsuffering), which are fruit of the Spirit. Lovingly deal with unruliness.

I am reminded of a group of male participants in a summer enhancement ministry at my church. One particular day, one of them began to call himself a Pharisee. The ministry was a day camp, so we were together all day. From time to time, I noticed that he was gathering more followers who would chant, "Pharisee, Pharisee, Pharisee." It sounded like members of a sorority, fraternity, or gang chanting the name of their group. It became a distraction, which they thought was amusing. I eventually got them together as a group during a break and asked what made them start that, directing the question to the ringleader. He very arrogantly let me know it was in the Bible. I gave them a homework assignment to find the word *Pharisee* in the Bible as many times as they could, read the situations, and tell me the next day who the Pharisees were. The behavior the next day was remarkably different. When I asked them halfway through the day, "What's a Pharisee?" the ringleader was the first to say, "I don't want to be one of them. Them guys was against Jesus." Unfortunately, that child found himself arrested in his later teen years on drug charges and received adult penalties. We had begun to instill the love of the Lord in him, but the street begged his attention.

If you cannot deal with a particular situation because it is it too hard, get help from a mentor, a seasoned saint. Brainstorm some strategies that others have used in your area to overcome victoriously the same type of problems you face. Your answer may be found in a person within or outside of your church family. Attend workshops held in your area and ask the questions that you need to have answered. When you do that in the Spirit of the Lord, God points you to the person with the word for you. Trust the gospel that you teach, or stop teaching! When high expectations are maintained and modeled by the leaders, the followers will be more in orderly. Accountability is crucial.

Help believers to develop emotional maturity for self-discipline. It has to start somewhere and there may not be anyone in the home modeling the behavior you think is appropriate. The child, the parent, and the grandparent exhibit the same behavior. Do not be judgmental; focus on the soul being won for the Lord. Discover strengths of the individual, and then use them for God's glory. Everyone is savable and everyone is teachable. Show that you care about them. Show students, how to praise the Lord for the gifts that have been freely given whatever the age. Lovingly point out where Scripture says this *gift* that they take for granted is an anointing from God created in them for God's purpose. In Jeremiah 29:11, we are reminded that God knows the plans or the thoughts that he has for each of us for good not for evil. *Show troubled believers the Word of God.* Remember that everyone is savable and they are in your class for a reason. Refrain from beating them over the head with the Bible; use it with meekness, gentleness, peace, patience, and love.

The enormity of the discipline factor diminishes when you secure in the gift of teaching that the Spirit has given you. Keep an open mind to learn from believers. Teaching is not a task; it is a gift. Using discipline strategies should become part of a perpetual process. A metamorphosis can occur for the teacher and student as they share God's truths in holistic ways.

How do you teach a Bible lesson that will assist believers with spiritual growth? **S**timulate, **m**otivate, **i**nvolve, and **l**ove them. Reach them with love. How does one teach a Bible lesson that enhances spiritual transfiguration? Help others develop self-discipline as you develop a variety of techniques that reflect the love of Jesus through your actions and the Word of God.

Using this method can yield positive discipline results. How? Self-discipline can lead to self-love. Are you limiting behaviors in others because you need limits in your own behaviors? Some teachers have spiritual issues that have never been addressed and are unknowingly in position to hinder the spiritual growth of others. Bible students need a teacher who is actively growing and modeling desired spiritual discipline. Many who are unprepared to teach have spiritually confused those wanting to learn. "If I could get them to be better than me ..." Change that approach. Ask God how he wants you to lovingly lead the process of spiritual growth. How can we lead where we are afraid to go?

Students say, "Reach me by loving me. But how can I accept your kind of love, when I cannot see that you love yourself? I see God's love because he wakes me up. I know Jesus loves me because he died for my sins. I accept the love of the Holy Spirit, which is in me. But the way I see you handling circumstances in your life makes me question it all."

Does the end (eternity) justify the means (my choice and yours to continue this Christian journey)? What happened to you that caused you not to love yourself? What can I do to avoid being a spiritual mess?

Why the discussion of discipline in this setting? *Reach Me with SMILES* is a handbook for developing disciple makers. You have read this far because you are a disciple who wants to assist other disciples to grow their relationship with the Lord. A disciple is a disciplined person. When you develop disciple makers, you are teaching Bible lessons and behaviors that you practice yourself. Others see growth in you and believe they can grow also.

Points to Ponder

Jesus calls us to action-oriented teaching ministries; God calls us to do his will. These come by way of spiritual self-discipline that precedes our efforts to lovingly lead others to follow Christ.

1. Develop spiritual discipline for yourself continuously.

2. Discipline yourself to study daily.

3. Dare to see *yourself* while studying. Don't just relate the Word to someone else.

4. Do not retreat, but use available resources to move to the next level of personal growth and development—whatever that is for you.

5. Learn to understand yourself and increase the love (acceptance) of self.

6. After self-reflection, you may be spiritually ready to lovingly lead others to a closer relationship with Christ. That's the heart of Christian discipline.

Rightly Dividing the Word

Habits and customs are routine behaviors practiced and developed over time. Jesus' disciples learned and practiced under his tutelage over a time period. Jesus once said that a student is not above his teacher; but everyone will be like his teacher, after he/she has been fully trained.

Reach me with love that looks like you have Jesus' joy or I am going to find another teacher. Will your students' next teacher be in the church house, the crack house, or the jailhouse? The people of God are no different from any other gathered group of people. We help make up our society, with all of its problems, and we bring the whole package with us to church; we are all sinners saved by God's grace. Christian educators and church leaders, what you say is important and what you do is important. You are responsible and accountable to God for how you divide his Word (2 Timothy 2:15). God's people are learning from what they see and hear from you. However, we must keep in mind that you cannot be responsible for their choices.

Christian educators must be obedient to the Word of God. We must be true to the content of our teaching; we must rightly divide the Word of truth. When we stray from the Word, we are vulnerable to consuming the bait of God's enemy. The bait is anything that separates us from the love of God and our ability to impart the Word of truth for Christ. How can we fish for men (Matthew 4:19) if we are not focused on the Father? Lift up the name of Jesus, even in the midst of what you deem to be negative behavior, and he will draw all unto himself.

We sometimes develop a slave mentality. We chain ourselves to a particular structure, tradition, custom, format, or just wanting so much to get through the material. We want to do what *we* want to do so badly we forget that we have prepared the material to get through to the people of God. If students do not hear the truth being taught in an age-appropriate manner, all kinds of problems may arise during teaching. These problems may appear at ages from children through senior adults. Rightly, or appropriately, divide the Word so that the Spirit of God can do its job of convicting the spirit of man, woman, boy or girl.

When people have problems understanding how to maintain discipline in their classrooms, they should immediately secure the Holy Scriptures as the key method of correction. Monthly, many churches read statements of faith (creeds or covenants) that bind them together as a body of believers in the same set of principles. In my church, it includes a part that says that we cultivate Christian courtesy and remember the rules of the Savior in the eighteenth chapter of Matthew. When we seriously accept that we are in covenant relationships, the way we demonstrate love is transformed. The routine, or habit, becomes seeking the best responses and reactions according to the biblical mandate, which never change.

Christian educators cannot afford to be easily angered by what some call "discipline problems" in the Christian classroom. James 1:19, 20 says that we must be quicker to hear and slower to speak. This refers us to hearing and doing the Word of God as examples or ambassadors even in the classroom. The way we react and respond may be the very image of godliness believers see that causes a cataclysmic change or life-altering decision to follow Christ Jesus as personal Lord and Savior. Not one of us is beyond the need for taking heed to James admonition to do what the Word says. We cannot forget what we are really like as well as what we used to be like. Someone modeled Christianity enough that we became followers. Make it the routine to exercise the spiritual fruit of patience, peace, and love while God does what is needed in the lives of believers.

Leading through Love

Teachers are leaders who need to be led by spiritually focused superintendents, pastors, and regional leaders. How do you teach a Bible lesson that will assist believers with spiritual growth? Love them enough to lead them by example. Many feelings and emotions arise when we talk about leadership that loves and how things ought to go. Each person has his or her own opinion based on something or other. However, when it comes to expressing thoughts, awkwardness sometimes appears. Teachers should be able to hold their leaders accountable just as the students should be able to hold the teachers accountable to being Christlike examples.

A leader can keep a finger on the pulse of the group through informal but written assessments to gather information. Surveys are one way of getting raw information and real answers to questions. Envision getting all that information in writing so it can be examined. How do you implement the ideas gleaned? It is important to take the time to think through what the participants have said in order to follow through meaningfully and effectively. Part of the process is to do something with the results. Or don't bother to solicit the information.

Sometimes, a survey is not appropriate when the Lord has spoken. As their spiritual leader, simply tell them that rather than soliciting opinions. If you have already firmly decided what and how you are going to do something but ask for opinions about it, you are setting up yourself and the ministry for failure regarding that. It introduces other leadership challenges when they hold it over your head that you asked, knowing you were going to do what you wanted to do regardless of their responses. Constant murmuring is loose, when all you needed to do was tell them what the Lord instructed you to do. The most important part of asking the right questions is listening and showing the people that you care about or value what they have to say. (See Appendix C and the section titled "Asking Questions that Stimulate Discussion.")

Conducting a survey provides a great source of information. However, some congregations have been overly surveyed. They are constantly asked for ideas and information, but little is done with the information collected. Following a survey, it is important to compile the information for the participants. They need to have a picture of what the survey implied and what will be done about the implications. In addition, be deliberate about finding ways to put into practice something as a direct result of the survey. If it was important enough to take the time to start the process, it is important enough to follow through. How valuable is simply *having* information? This could be the springboard for your next class session, meeting, or personal study and spiritual growth.

Point to Ponder

Read the Scriptures below that will help you to stay rooted in your purpose.

Mark 10:35–44   to serve

Philippians 2:5–8   with humility

Barbara A. F. Brehon

1 Peter 4:7–10   with servant love

Practice

Show love first in your home.

Show love everywhere you go.

For Further Reading

Ryken, Leland et al. gen. ed. *Dictionary of Biblical Imagery.* Downers

Grove, Illinois: InterVarisity Press, 1998.

The New National Baptist Hymnal, Nashville: National Baptist

Publishing Board, 1974.

Encourage

Reach out to me.
Encourage my reconciliation to the Savior.
Lift me when I slip a little or fall.

Encourage

How do you teach a Bible lesson that will assist believers with spiritual growth? The teacher should stimulate, **m**otivate, **i**nvolve, **l**ove, **e**ncourage, and **s**trengthen all believers. The believers who come to us are saying, "Reach me by encouraging me." When a person becomes an active participant in a local congregation, their journey is beginning, not ending. The care, time, and concern that were shown when the Word was presented to them must be continued. Someone somewhere invited them to your place of worship or to your class. How do you keep them? You must **SMILE**. You cannot help them grow if you cannot keep them encouraged.

When Barnabas arrived in Antioch and saw the evidence of the grace of God, he encouraged the people (Acts 11:22–23). The writer of Hebrews reminded his audience of their confidence in Christ, the hope they professed, and the need to exhort or to encourage one another toward love (10:19–25). Whatever keeps you involved and motivated may be the key to keeping others encouraged. Develop new strategies for keeping people. Look introspectively for answers to the following questions that will assist you in this part of your growth and development.

What keeps you involved in the church?

What makes you want to quit sometimes?

What can be done to prevent you from wanting to quit sometimes?

Who is responsible for preventing you from dropping out?

Why do we want the church to grow?

(See Appendix C.)

Teaching in Diversity

Teaching is a spiritual gift (Romans 12:6–8; 1 Corinthians 12:28–30). That gift assists Christians with making disciples of others who have accepted Christ as their personal Lord and Savior. Teaching helps Christians explain the gospel to others in order for them to make the decision to accept Jesus. *Merriam-Webster's Collegiate Dictionary* gives several definitions of the verb *teach*: to cause to know a subject; to cause to know how; to accustom to some action or attitude; to make to know the disagreeable consequences of some action; to guide; to impart knowledge; to seek to make known and accepted.

Scripture says that there are diversities of gifts given to the body of believers in Jesus; one of those gifts is the teaching. **Diversity** is the condition of being different or having differences. People are innately different from one another. Being diverse means we are unlike each other and have various forms or qualities. This is *Merriam-Webster's Collegiate Dictionary's* way of defining diversity. Additionally, a

Christian should define it as a necessity and characteristic of the church where Jesus Christ is the head. Though more than one person in a particular body of believers would have the same spiritual gift, individuals within the body provide opportunities to minister to the needs of the entire body.

Christian educators must see teaching through the lens of the Holy Bible. Jesus **taught** the multitude many things (Mark 6:34). Barnabas and Saul **taught** in the early church (Acts 11:25–26). In Colossians 2:6–7, people had received Christ and were being admonished to walk in him, being rooted firmly, built up in him, and established in faith just as they had been **instructed**. The term in these passages comes from the Greek word *didasko*,[3] which means to instruct by word of mouth; to influence the understanding of the person who is taught; as instruction in the Christian faith and Christian teaching. The same form of this word is found in Romans 12:7 and Hebrews 5:12.

God appointed teachers in the church (1 Corinthians 12:28). Since this statement appears amidst the discussion of the gifts of the spirit for the common good of the body, we know that we should have persons teaching whom the Holy Spirit gifts for that ministry, in Jesus' name. Are people who are not gifted to teach by the Holy Spirit teaching the Word of God in our churches? We should not become so diverse in our local churches that we continue to allow this to be. Our educational ministries must not continue to function in our churches differently from what is mandated in God's Word. 1 Corinthians 12:4 tells us that there are varieties of gifts but one Spirit. Verse 11 says that the Holy Spirit is the one who distributes (divides or classifies) those gifts individually as the Spirit wills. Those who have the spiritual gift of teaching must be the teachers in our churches.

We must look at the teachers on our staffs and hold them accountable for recognizing whether or not they are gifted by the Holy Spirit to teach. The fact that a person teaches in the school system or conducts training programs for their profession does not necessarily make them the best pick for a teacher of the Word of God. While it is true that such persons can use their abilities in the name of Jesus, we must select teachers with giftedness as the priority. (I want to remind you that I have secular teacher training. I am not bashing schoolteachers; I am one. I want to emphasize that the professional teacher and the spiritually gifted teacher may not be one in the same.)

We must also look at learners as a diverse group and become person minded in our teaching. Diversity in the body of Christ is a part of the description of the body. We must recognize the importance of our differences and teach to the differences that are assembled in the learning environments that God allows us to provide. (Review the sections titled "Stimulate" and "Motivate.") The Spirit of God gives unity to the body; we are not trying to teach everyone the same way, nor should we look upon each other as though all are the same.

Scripture confirms that we were created to be spiritually different for the common good of the fellowship of believers of which we are a part.

Encouragement must be a vital part of the lessons we impart as Christian teachers. Knowing our subject or curriculum is not enough; encouragement is affirming others in their walk with the Lord. Christians give encouragement to show that they value and appreciate the worth of another individual. How do you teach a Bible lesson that will assist believers with spiritual growth? Assure them that they have the ability and the spiritual capacity to use their God-given gifts to enlighten the corner of the world in which they reside. Not everyone can identify with everyone else. However, individuals speak to the needs of certain persons because they reflect something familiar. God made us in his image and gifted us so that we glorify him. Within the context of our experiences, we minister to the needs of others that God places along our path. He gives us what we need in order to speak truth to those we encounter.

The Holy Spirit is a gift from God that we receive when we become born-again believers in Jesus Christ. The Holy Spirit deposits within us a special gift from God that is to be used to edify others for the uplifting of the kingdom of God. Each Christian is gifted in a particular way for his local congregation for the work of that congregation in meeting the particular needs of the community (Ephesians 4:11–12).

We need to refresh our teaching strategies to include the reality of the diversity of believers in the body of Christ. We can take comfort in knowing that God joins the members of the body together and can revitalize us as we accept, affirm, and encourage others to be their authentic selves in Christ.

There is beauty in the diversity of the body of believers in the Lord Jesus Christ. When we preach and teach God's truth, the gospel of Jesus Christ, the Lord adds to the church. At that point, persons need to be discipled; he needs to be taught the Word of God for righteous living. This teaching needs to be in the context or in the reality of who the persons are or who they have been created by God to be as defined by their giftedness. We must make disciples by helping people discover and use their spiritual gifts, knowing that gifts from God are not the same things as talent people in the world possess.

Using Gifts for Disciple Making

One of the roles of the teacher in making disciples is reaching people where they are. Helping them to see that who they are is why God can use them. It is because of the gifts they have and the experiences they have collected that someone else will come to know the Lord through them. The gift helps to determine and define the method a person uses to be an effective witness. Each person is needed to reach someone else and Christian teachers need to be encouragers so that the testimony of those they teach will be vital to the growth of the church. Barnabas was sent out by the church in Jerusalem to Antioch to verify the growth of the church among the Gentiles. When he saw the grace of God, he was glad and encouraged them all that with purpose of heart they should continue with the Lord (Acts 11:22–23). Help others to know they have a purpose in Christ.

Discipleship can take place in any forum where the Word of God is studied. As believers mature as disciples, we must encourage them to become disciple makers. Teachers are encouragers who see the value in diversity for kingdom building. We are responsible for equipping people to disciple others and must therefore recognize the diversity that comes with the body having many members (1 Corinthians 12). The ministry of the teacher includes embracing all and finding creative ways to reach all for Christ. It is at this point that we become teachers for spiritual transformation into the very likeness of Christ. How did Jesus teach? He knew what methods to use for each situation to convey the same message. He understood the context of his ministry; Jesus was a disciple maker who embraced diversity.

To each one of us, grace was given according to the measure or amount of Christ's gift, the Holy Spirit. The Greek term being used here for Christ (*Christos*) means "anointed" (Ephesians 4:7). In other words, being gifted means being anointed. We must acknowledge God's ability to anoint whomever he wants to anoint with the gift that he wants them to have. As a disciple maker, help others to understand that they have a measure or capacity for the gifts they have. We are gifted diversely, or in your own way, to equip the saints for service to build up Christ's body. The whole body is fitted together and properly joined by every member of the body. The proper working of each part causes growth (Ephesians 4:1–16). Therefore, we must encourage people to grow according to the measure of their giftedness. We must accept them as they are. Once we evangelize and bring them into our fellowship, we must help them move to the next spiritual level as we move to our next level by using our gifts as teacher/encourager.

We can help others to know where and how they fit into the church body. Christian educators must help others with an understanding of why gifts are given at the time of conversion and allow time for a discussion of their individual gifts for the common good (1 Corinthians 12). Make time available for them to share where and how they fit into the ministry of the local church. This will assist the fulfillment of individual callings to do service in the name of Jesus.

I have assumed that those who are reading this and serving as Christian educators in their local churches have discovered, developed, and deployed their gifts. It is unfortunate but true that some leaders in our churches do not have a clue what their own gifts are. For that matter, when you mention gifts, some leaders do not think of spiritual gifts as listed in the Bible. I chaired a committee at another local church. I began by surveying the strengths and weaknesses of the persons appointed by the pastor to serve. To my surprise, they listed all kinds of things as gifts they brought to the table. I handed those surveys to the pastor and chose another route of assessment. The pastor decided to revisit the teaching of gifts to the congregation though that pastor had previously addressed it.

The question is not only whether or not we have teachers teaching who are not gifted to teach, but do we have leaders leading who do not have the gift of administration or the understanding of leading a gift-based ministry?

Christian educators must help others to understand the need to be good stewards of gifts (1 Peter 4:10–11). As applied to the apostles, ministers of the gospel, and private believers, *steward* refers to a person who manages domestic affairs, originating from the Greek word *oikonomos*. As servants of our Lord Jesus, we serve by the strength that God supplies to the measure the Holy Spirit gives us individually. Teachers, then, help others to see this as a means of glorifying God through Christ. We must also learn and teach about spiritual gifts because God does not want us to be ignorant.

We must **teach everyone**, without exclusion, so that they are presented complete before Christ (Colossians 1:28). Become true disciples so that what follows is disciple making.

Points to Ponder

List your spiritual gifts.

How are your spiritual gifts being used to benefit your local congregation?

Name at least three individuals you have assisted with spiritual growth within the last six months. (Your personal relationship with them helps your assessment.)

Practice

What will you do within the next three months to demonstrate your commitment to being an effective disciple maker? How will you **SMILE**?

Stimulate others:

Motivate others:

Involve others:

Love others:

Encourage others:

For Further Reading

Garner, Larry and Tony Martin, *Gifts of Grace: Discovering and Using Your Spiritual Gifts*. Jackson, Mississippi: Baptist Books, 1995.

Johnston, Jay and Ronald Brown. *Teaching the Jesus Way: Building a Transformational Teaching Ministry*. Nashville: LifeWay Press, 2000.

Zodhiates, Spiros, ed. *The Hebrew-Greek Key Word Study Bible* (NASB). Chattanooga: AMG Publishers, 1998.

Strengthen

Reach out to me.
Strengthen me with your energy. Uphold me by
being present with me when I am in need.

Strengthen

The Christian approach to teaching establishes a base for each lesson that is derived from self-directed and continual personal study. The final aspect of the SMILES concept reminds us that our approach toward Christian teaching has to be sound. The theoretical foundation must evolve out of your personal experience with the Lord and must comprise the belief system rooted in Christian convictions. Self-evaluation or self-examination is expected; recognize self and see whether you are in the faith (2 Corinthians 13:5). Can you say, "I recognize that I am a part of Christ because he lives in me?" When Jesus lives in you daily and you continue to prepare to teach others, you know that you **s**timulate, **m**otivate, **i**nvolve, **l**ove, **e**ncourage, and **s**trengthen others. Your students may be spiritually fragile and need your strength.

How do you teach a Bible lesson that will assist believers with spiritual growth? Believers come to us saying, "Reach me by strengthening me." Know that one of your roles is to edify the body of believers. Be a spiritual bodybuilder. Ephesians 4:11–16 tells us that Christ gave some to be teachers so that they could prepare God's people for service. In order to serve Christ, we must be edified, built up, or strengthened. We must become mature Christians ourselves and then assist others in attaining the measure of the fullness of Christ. That reminds me of safety instructions reviewed before any airline takes flight. "Be sure to secure your oxygen mask before assisting others."

Each of us must continue to grow in God's grace in the unity of the Holy Spirit joined together and held together by Christ, the head of the body of believers. As we build up others who grow and mature in the Word, they learn to build up still others who grow. Thus, each person does his or her part according to the spirit that works within.

We must be open; we must be willing to discover, uncover, and recover all that keeps us pointed in Christ's direction. We must not cover ourselves up with anything except the banner of Jesus. We find in Christ the strength that helps us to reach others for Christ. People on a faith quest will recognize the spirit and be drawn to the Christ that lives within us. Then we become obligated to edify the learners or strengthen them for remainder of the Christian journey. The lessons we plan to teach should strengthen our students for life's journey. The spiritual maturity level for students in any class is diverse. When you finish your lesson, will believers be able to see and feel the Lord in it? Will those who are yet uncertain be drawn closer to a heartfelt decision for Christ? If they can, you have strengthened them.

Moving beyond Discipleship

Discipleship is personal; it is about *me* and *my* relationship with the Lord. Disciple making takes discipleship to the next level. We have a personal relationship with the Lord as a disciple and we grow because of discipleship, the process of learning to be like Jesus. Now that we are maturing in our faith, we reproduce others who want to know Jesus and desire a closer relationship with the Father. We move from simply being a Christian to going out, searching for, and satisfying the needs of others. They come to know who God is through Christ. That's disciple making. Disciple makers want to cultivate hearts for Christ. When we make disciples, we are about building God's kingdom. So the question is this: are you growing? Are you growing spiritually? In what way is growth occurring? Are you changing, and is that change moving you in the right direction—toward God?

Point to Ponder

Read Acts 17 and think about how Paul made disciples. Using the entire chapter, list action words that show what he did. Notice the pattern that emerges. (Note that in 16:37, Paul is included in "they." Start with verse 1.) Remember to only list the words that show action, such as *had passed, came, traveled,* and *reasoned.*

Making Disciples

The word *disciple* is used once in the Old Testament and more than two hundred times in the New Testament (Isaiah 8:16, Matthew, Mark, Luke, John, Acts, 1 Corinthians, and Galatians). The phrase "make disciples" is used once in the Bible, Matthew 28:19–20.

What is a disciple? It is a follower, a learner, a student.

What is discipleship? Discipleship is the process of learning to be a follower of Jesus Christ. It involves building a personal relationship with Jesus that requires time studying the Word of God, praying to God, and exercising your spiritual gifts.

What is a disciple maker? A disciple maker is one who teaches others the things that Jesus commanded and how to observe them.

How do you make disciples? Teach them! Teach them to observe the things commanded by God. Disciples share the Word of God and produce fruit. As you exercise your gift, you produce fruit of the spirit. (Galatians 5:22–23). An apple tree produces apples. A pear tree produces pears. A fig tree produces figs. A disciple maker produces other disciples. (John 15:4–8). Disciple makers help others to see their need to be in a growing relationship with God.

What is the difference between discipleship and disciple making? Discipleship is personal and occurs when an individual has decided to follow a model or particular set of beliefs. Disciple making involves teaching others. It happens when an individual is intentional about helping others to not only choose to be a follower but also grow. Disciple making is a process that begins with a plan. We must count the cost, which includes time, energy, and emotional involvement. Then, we must proceed in decency and order (1 Corinthians 14:40) and cut the confusion being attentive to edification and strengthening the body of believers. Jesus said he would build his church upon a rock. (Matthew 16:18). Each Christian is a rock upon which the church (universal) has been built. Read and study the Bible to grow closer to God.

Disciple making takes discipleship to the next level. When we make disciples, we are building God's kingdom. We have a personal relationship with the Lord as a disciple and we grow because of discipleship, the process of learning to be like Jesus. Humbly and peacefully accept the Word of God when you read it, especially when it makes you feel awkward and uncomfortable. I agree with a statement that I read in *First Steps to Understanding Your Bible* by James M. Gray. He wrote that we must not be too proud to learn or to obey what we read, although such obedience may be difficult at times. Receive the Word planted as a seed put in fertile soil that will gently sprout. Let the Word blossom in you because it will save you when you let it grow.

Barbara A. F. Brehon

Planning for Disciple Making

Effective Christian educators understand and accept that the gift of teaching is not all about themselves. This is not the place for you to be self-absorbed. Romans 12:3 reminds us not to think too highly of ourselves but to have sound judgment. Good judgment helps our prayers evolve around others rather than self. What *we* want is not the focus. We begin to hunger and thirst after righteousness. (Matthew 5:6).

1. Don't be angry or despondent when you don't get what you expect. It doesn't get to be about you.

2. Don't lose heart, for your inner man is renewed daily while the outer man decays (2 Corinthians 4:16–18).

3. Don't fear failure or criticism. Our adequacy comes from God (2 Corinthians 3:5).

4. Your highest aim should not be self-fulfillment. When you lose your life for Jesus, you save it (Luke 9:24).

5. **The Ultimate Goal**: How does this glorify God?

   How does my ministry involvement glorify God?

   Does it minister to the Lord?

   Does it minister to the saint?

   Does it minister to the sinner?

   Does it conquer Satan and his kingdom?

Increasing Teacher Effectiveness

Sometimes, problems or challenges do arise in the area of **staffing.** The nature of volunteerism, untrained and non-gifted teachers, and inadequate curriculum can become thorns in the flesh of the Christian educator. Volunteers are not always dedicated to making long-term commitments. Therefore, specifying short-term appointments (thirteen weeks, one year) might help. The short term could be for a regular class or a special emphasis topic. When the person sees that the responsibility terminates at a designated time, the commitment could become firm. You know when the term expires, which gives you time to explore the next step: the same teacher, another teacher, or another topic. You could have a team of teachers that rotate being the lead teacher each quarter. Each teacher has the chance to sit with another person teaching the same class. The observations from the student's point of view could prove to be very valuable. The opportunity is built in for the volunteers to rededicate themselves at the end of that quarter/year or use the gifts they have in another area of Christian ministry.

That phase becomes a growth tool for personal development and discovery. The Christian educator does not know the conversations the volunteer has had with the Lord. They may have grown to something else, leaving that slot open for someone who has grown for it. No position is etched in concrete and is subject to growth, change. Positions don't belong to individuals. The church benefits when its members recognize whether or not God has called them to work in specific areas.

Untrained teachers may become frustrated. They may feel that the curriculum is inadequate and burn out before becoming equipped. Spiritual mentors can be helpful. One person becomes available to assist in the new teacher's development. Being able to ask questions, discuss ideas, and air reasons for frustration are important parts of growth. Mentor someone in an effort to edify and affirm him or her. Strengthening him or her strengthens the students. As you share teaching techniques, all people grow. Be a body builder spiritually. Position yourself so that you bear fruit that is portable; you can take it wherever you go. Imagine its effect on believers as they learn by observing this process of sharing. After all, we are commanded to go and tell others. We are not supposed to keep what God has given us to ourselves. By reaching one, we reach others.

Increasing your own effectiveness is a by-product of helping others, but it also presents **challenges**. The first challenge is to know self. Who are you and what is it that you like to do? Hold on to that thought. I challenge you to come up with a way that God can use it. Although your first thought may not be *a religious thing per se,* God can still use it. If God gets the glory out of it, then it can be a benefit of God's kingdom. How do you use what you like to do effectively for the ministry of Christ? Each person must authentically work with the gifts they possess, together with the gifts of others to benefit the kingdom. Nothing is a small thing; the gift is what you are to do in the name of the Lord. Do all things as if you are doing it for him. Think of how the best artisans were told to create a certain thing in making the tent of meeting and religious paraphernalia in Exodus. God told Moses exactly what to make, how to make, and whom to choose to make it. One was best at working with fabric, another gold, another wood, etc. What is it that you truly like to do? How can you use it for the ministry of Christ? When you poll the staff in search of their answers to such questions, service projects promoted by the education ministry emerge. Different classes or groups develop project ideas that fit their gifts. A person to coordinate the education ministry projects will also emerge. People using skills and gifts they enjoy remain loyal longer.

Think of the last lesson you taught or the last lesson that someone taught to you. What did the main person in this lesson do? How can you look back over the past week and show a specific example of where you demonstrated that trait in your own life? Or was there an opportunity that you missed? Daily reflections become the food for fruitfulness, a by-product of Christian teaching.

Therefore, a second challenge one encounters when trying to become more effective is personal application. The teacher can become so busy preparing to teach that the private connection of biblical messages is lost week after week. We must faithfully allow the Holy Spirit to reveal something in our lives that demonstrates his presence. Experience the difference between how you felt about the last lesson you taught and how you felt when it connected it back to you. If you are really teaching, you are trying to effectuate or facilitate a change in the believers. Use the Bible as a tool to get the Word stirred up in people, but until you use it personally, what have you done? Make sure that the Word feeds you before thinking about how it is going to feed your students.

A third challenge is to share self. Find someone with whom you are already comfortable, a person with whom you can share yourself within the sphere of who you are. Look at where you go every day and to whom you talk. As you avail yourself to others, God moves more mightily in your life. Discover that all of life's daily experiences become a part of teaching.

A fourth and often overlooked challenge is ministering to those with special needs. Almost every congregation has someone who exhibits limited mental or physical capacity. How are their spiritual needs met and nurtured? I submit to you the entire SMILES concept. Everything that has been written here includes Christians with low functioning abilities. When you dare to treat them with the same concern you show others, their response with be growth to the ability level God has given them. We are *all* fearfully and wonderfully made. (Psalm 139:14). Those with special needs are also able to know God and deserve your SMILES. Someone with a certain gift is waiting for the opportunity to share a portion of himself or herself in just that manner. Seek them. Let them.

I remember telling a friend about a special need for a deaf and mute member of the church. As an audiologist, she knew exactly what to do. A sign language ministry emerged that assisted the young man, his family, and others of all ages in the congregation and community. Many people learned to sign and it was incorporated into the praise dancing as well. Love them, lead them, and feed them.

Summary

Increasing teacher effectiveness is a never-ending process. Reaching out to mentor another uncovers what people need because you are hearing them. You may need to come up with classes that have not previously existed in your church to meet the current needs of the congregation. If there is not a vehicle in the church to minister to an expressed need, develop it so that the people can be fully fed. If you are not going to respond with action, there is no need to listen.

As you journey through the Bible, make it apply to your own life. Otherwise, how can you teach it?

Teacher effectiveness is a by-product of helping others to grow spiritually, and it presents challenges. As we strengthen others, we must remember to strengthen ourselves and stay rooted in the Word.

We must not let our thinking deter us from obedience to the Great Commission. People need to feel that someone cares about what happens to them. They need to feel that they are wanted, that they belong, and that they are needed. Strengthen them.

Point to Ponder

List key ideas that are important factors for teachers.

Now, go forth and teach "all nations."

Studying the Word of God

In order to participate in the process of being transformed into the image of Jesus Christ, Christians must study the Word of God. Ministry must be committed to the growth and development of Christians. Do you have a desire to live and keep God's Word? Is your prayer like the psalmist who prayed for his eyes to be open? (Psalm 119:18). Studying the Word of God to attain spiritual knowledge from

God is expected. We should study the Bible with diligence, humility, and prayer.

Prayerfully enter the study of God's Word so that you hear God. Allow the Holy Spirit to be manifested. Whether you are at home, on a break at work, or at school, be intentional about how you enter the presence of the Lord. The time that you set aside to study the Bible is important. Plan time to pray before you read the Word to prepare your heart and mind; pray while you study to ensure the purity of your thoughts. Also, plan enough time to pray after you have sat with the Word so that you hear God and internalize his truths. Avoid being rushed with your study.

Here are some suggestions of ways to study God's Word: with diligence, desire, dependence, and discipline. **Diligence** in studying the Word of God requires desire, dependence, and discipline from you. They are prerequisites to the effective and diligent Bible study of every believer. In Acts 17:11, the people of Berea received the word with all readiness and searched the Word daily to discover truth.

Our **desire** for God strengthens us. James 4:8 tells us that we must submit to God. When we yield to God and resist the devil, the enemy will flee from us. We must want to be in God's company. God draws near to us as we draw near to him. We have to want to stop doing things that are not pleasing to him. We metaphorically cleanse our hands of things we used to do because of a desire to please God.

When we purify our hearts, our desires turn to wanting to know what he wants us to know and what he wants us to do. Christians are blessed when we hunger for the Lord. (Matthew 5:6).

Another prerequisite for Bible study is **dependence** upon the Holy Spirit. John 14:26 tells us that the Holy Spirit will teach us all things. Additionally, 1 Corinthians 2:10–13 tells us that God reveals through his Spirit the things that he has prepared for those who love him. Since we cannot know the mind of God, we must depend on the Holy Spirit to help us understand the things of God. We have received the Spirit, who is from God, so that we might know the things that have been freely given to us by God. We must study so that our speech is not man's wisdom but God's. There are times when being dependent strengthens us. The idea of dependence being a weakness is worldly. We must depend on God.

Therefore, **discipline** in applying yourself to the study of the Word is another prerequisite to diligence in studying the Bible. Paul told Timothy to charge the people not to strive about words to no profit but to be diligent to present themselves to God (2 Timothy 2:14–15). In other words, study in such a manner that will please God when you share the Word accurately with others. This way, you have nothing of which to be ashamed. Discipline strengthens.

Point to Ponder

Read all of Psalm 119 and meditate on it. Journal your thoughts.

Study the Bible with the kind of gratitude that makes you thankful daily just to have it and to be able to share time with God. When we value something, we hold it in high esteem. Its importance can be seen in our thankfulness for having it. Our gratitude gives it a place of significance because it is worth something to us. What is the revival of your soul worth to you? The law of the Lord revives the soul and gives joy to the heart. Do you consider the Bible more precious than gold and sweeter than honey from the honeycomb (Psalm 19:10)? The reward in keeping the ordinances of God is great.

Reading the Word of God

The way we read and the way we study are not the same. Turn your attention to reading the Word of God for all its worth.

Seven Comparisons

1. When Christians read the Bible, they comprehend what the words say.

    When you study, the Holy Spirit is teaching you while you read.

2. When Christians read the Bible, they understand writings.

    When you study, you gain knowledge of the truths of God.

3. When Christians read the Bible, they convert what they see into meaning by relating it to their own experiences.

   When you study, you scrutinize what is being said in the text.

4. When Christians read the Bible, they glance at the surface of words.

   When you study, you research, or do word studies, digging for deeper spiritual meanings.

5. When Christians read the Bible, they may recite what has been said.

   When you study, you consider reasons why it was probably stated that way.

6. When Christians read the Bible, they scan for particular words to trigger something within.

   When you study, you carefully look at every word and wait for the Holy Spirit to speak through every nuance or fine distinction in usage from one version and language to another.

7. When Christians read the Bible, they examine the words in relation to the words around it, one kind of context.

   When you study, you examine the passage before and after the one you have read, according to the big pictures that God shows you (biblical context).

Reading requires skills of seeing and pronouncing words in relation to a particular context. Without the context, the words have no meaning and reading does not take place; we are merely looking at the words and calling them something. We need to look at the words of Scripture and come away with what God is saying, what the passage means, and how we can use it in our lives for the glory of God for the entire world to see. Observe. Interpret. Apply. Therefore, we must improve our basic reading skills while we are reading the Word of God so that we get what God is trying to tell us.

Are you a disciple or a disciple maker? Or are you both? As a disciple, you strengthen your individual relationship with God through Jesus Christ. As a disciple maker, you help others to learn about Jesus and you teach them to obey all that Jesus commanded (Matthew 28:19–20) while you continually strengthen your personal relationship with the Lord. Understanding this distinction will help you to strengthen others in the name of Jesus.

An article titled "Removing the Training Wheels" in the *Discipleship Journal* (January/February 2003) raised an important question. How do you help those you are discipling begin ministering to others? My thoughts turned to another question. How many of us are ready to move to another level in our service but won't because of insecurity or apprehension of failing?

A Final Point to Ponder

Have you been discipled repeatedly and just cannot see how God could use you to minister to others? When you are spiritually mature enough to begin ministering to others, you see the needs of others. Keep it simple, saints (KISS), by taking small steps that you can handle, and stay connected to a spiritual mentor. I pray for opportunities for each of us to grow in our walk with God, individually and as disciples who make other disciples.

While you wait for God to develop you, be faithful in prayer. Be patient with those you disciple as God was with you. Do not give up on them. Be diligent in prayer and be available as an instrument of God.

God will deliver you and God will discipline you; these two things work together to develop you into disciples that will be focused on the Father. He wants us to be so committed to him that we fulfill the Great Commission of Christ. "Go and make disciples." However, before you can make one, you have to be one. If you are seeking self-gratification and glory through what you do and say, get ready to be disciplined.

While studying the book of Isaiah, I was struck by God's promise to preserve the survivors of the Assyrian and Babylonian exiles who honored and praised him. Isaiah wanted to know how long he would have to prophesy to God's people. He was purposely sent on a mission to a people who would not listen. God told him to prophesy until great desolation had occurred (Isaiah 6:8–13). God will not continue to let you distract his people. He got tired of the sin of the Israelites. Woe to them who do such. Are your methods for disciple making developing persons who actually go forth and make other disciples? Are you a disciple maker producing fruit, other disciple makers?

Oh, Lord, am I distracting your people, blurring their vision of you? Do the words that I speak draw others to you or to my issues? Lord, are my actions pleasing to you, or are they barriers that block your blessings from those who would otherwise become disciples and makers of disciples? Deliver me, Lord, from myself. Discipline me, Lord, so I can learn from you. Develop me into the disciple maker that you have commissioned me to be. Nurture me, Lord, so that I may help others to grow closer to you as I grow closer to you. Nurture me, Lord, while I wait to see you in eternity. Patiently wait for the Lord. (Psalm 40:1–4).

Share the Gospel of Jesus Christ! (John 3:16–17)

For Further Reading

Gray, James M. *First Steps to Understanding Your Bible*. Chicago: Meridian Publication, 1996.

Epilogue

The urgency and seriousness of your conviction to being *called* to teach, to make disciples, is an awesome responsibility. Know who you are. Know your purpose. And know what you are teaching. Read, observe, interpret, and apply Scripture by considering the context of the passage; read what comes before and after it. Always consider preparation for teaching as a process and develop methods and activities to lift the central theme or single concept to be taught for that lesson. Repeating the learning process is crucial.

Furthermore, know the people you are teaching. Keep your lessons fresh; stay equipped and current with what God has called you to do. Read and attend training sessions locally, statewide, and nationally when possible. Stay abreast of methods and materials to remain current, and vary the techniques you employ for teaching and learning based on the goal or objective of the passage at hand. Self-evaluate regularly, and have confidence. Know that Jesus is able to keep you from falling, as you reach the children of God with SMILES.

How do you teach a Bible lesson that will assist believers with spiritual growth?

With SMILES!

Stimulate	me.
Motivate	me.
Involve	me.
Love	me.
Encourage	me.
Strengthen	me.

Do this and you will reach me for Christ!

References

Anderson, Lorin W. ed. *International Encyclopedia of Teaching and Teacher Education*. Pergamon, 1995.

Armstrong, Thomas. "Multiple Intelligences in the Classroom," *Association for Supervision and Curriculum Development*, 2000.

Arn, Win and Charles Arn. *The Master's Plan for Making Disciples: Every Christian an Effective Witness through an Enabling Church*. Grand Rapids, Michigan: Baker Books, 1998.

Anderson, Andy. *The Growth Spiral*. Nashville: Broadman and Holman Publishers, 1993.

Johnston, Jay and Ronald Brown. *Teaching the Jesus Way: Building a Transformational Teaching Ministry*. Nashville: LifeWay Press, 2000.

Campbell, Roger. *Staying Positive in a Negative World: Attitudes That Enhance the Joy of Living*, Grand Rapids, Michigan: Kregel Publications, 1997.

Carlson, Gregory C. *Understanding Teaching: Effective Biblical Teaching*. Wheaton, Illinois: Evangelical Training Association, 1998.

Edge, Findley B. *Teaching for Results*. Nashville: Broadman and Holman Publishers, 1995.

Foster, Charles R. *The Future of Christian Education. Educating Congregations.* Nashville: Abingdon Press, 1994.

Fitch, James E. *Building a Great Church through the Sunday School,* Nashville: Convention Press, 1993.

Garner, Larry and Tony Martin, *Gifts of Grace: Discovering and Using Your Spiritual Gifts* Jackson, Mississippi: Baptist Books, 1995.

Gray, James M. *First Steps to Understanding Your Bible.* Chicago: Meridian Publications, 1996.

Griggs, Donald L. and Judy M. Walther. *Christian Education in the Small Church,* Valley Forge, Pennsylvania: Judson Press, 1992.

Halverson, Delia. *32 Ways to Become a Great Sunday School Teacher.* Nashville: Abingdon Press, 1997.

Hammett, Edward H. *The Gathered and Scattered Church: Equipping Believers for the 21st Century.* Macon, Georgia: Smyth and Helwys, 1999.

Hawkins, Don. *Master Discipleship: Jesus' Prayer and Plan for Every Believer.* Grand Rapids, Michigan: Kregel Resources, 1996.

Hawkins, O. S. *Drawing the Net: 30 Practical Principles for Leading Others to Christ Publicly and Personally.* Nashville: Broadman Press, 1993.

Hemphill, Ken. *Revitalizing the Sunday Morning Dinosaur: A Sunday School Growth Strategy for the 21st Century.* Nashville: Broadman and Holman Publishers, 1996.

Henderson, David W. *Culture Shift: Communicating God's Truth to Our Changing World*. Grand Rapids, Michigan: Baker Books, 1999.

Henrichsen, Walter A. *Disciples Are Made Not Born: Equipping Christians to Multiply Themselves through Ministry to Others*. Colorado Springs, Colorado: Chariot Victor Publishing, 1988.

Lingo, Susan L. *Larger-than-Life Activities: Colossal Crafts That Teach and Serve*. Cincinnati: The Standard Publishing Company, 1998.

Malphurs, Aubrey. *Strategy 2000: Churches Making Disciples for the Next Millennium*. Grand Rapids, Michigan: Kregel Publications, 1996.

McCaleb, George. *Stir Up the Gifts*. Lithonia, Georgia: Orman Press, 1999.

McQuay, Earl P. *Learning to Study the Bible*. Nashville: Broadman Press, 1992.

Mims, Gene. *Kingdom Principles for Church Growth*. Nashville: Convention Press, 1994.

Nanus, Burt. *Leading the Way to Organization Renewal*. Portland, Oregon: Productivity Press, 1996.

Orlich, Donald C. et al. *Teaching Strategies: A Guide to Better Instruction*. D. C. Heath, 1980.

Roehlkepartain, Eugene C. *The Teaching Church: Moving Christian Education to Center Stage*. Nashville: Abingdon Press, 1993.

Ryken, Leland et al. Gen. ed. *Dictionary of Biblical Imagery*. Downers Grove, Illinois: InterVarisity Press, 1998.

Schaller, Lyle E. *21 Bridges to the 21st Century: The Future of Pastoral Ministry*. Nashville: Abingdon Press, 1994.

Shawchuck, Norman and Gustave Rath. *Benchmarks of Quality in the Church: 21 Ways to Continuously Improve the Content of Your Ministry*. Nashville: Abingdon Press, 1994.

Smith, Donald P. *How to Attract and Keep Active Church Members*. Louisville: John Knox Press, 1992.

Stewart, Carlyle F. *African American Church Growth: 12 Principles for Prophetic Ministry*. Nashville: Abingdon Press, 1994.

Taylor, Bill L. *21 Truths, Traditions, and Trends: Propelling the Sunday School into the 21st Century*. Nashville: Convention Press, 1996.

The New National Baptist Hymnal. Nashville: National Baptist Publishing Board, 1974.

Warren, Rick. *The Purpose Driven Church: Growth without Compromising Your Message and Mission*. Grand Rapids, Michigan: Zondervan Publishing House, 1995.

Welch, Bobby H. *Evangelism through the Sunday School: A Journey of Faith*. Nashville: LifeWay Press, 1997.

Wilhoit, Jim and Leland Ryken. *Effective Bible Teaching*. Grand Rapids, Michigan: Baker Book House, 1995.

Willis, Avery Jr., *MasterLife*. Nashville: LifeWay.

Yount, William R. *Called to Teach: An Introduction to the Ministry of Teaching.* Nashville: Broadman and Holman Publishers, 1999.

Wimberly, Anne Streaty. *Soul Stories: African American Christian Education.* Nashville: Abingdon Press, 1994.

Zodhiates, Spiros. *The Hebrew-Greek Key Word Study Bible* (NASB). Chattanooga: AMG Publishers, 1998.

Appendix A

Suggested Learning Activities to Enhance Reaching Believers for Lasting Spiritual Growth

- Book of the Bible Book Review
- Sensory Images from Sensory Details
- Reading the Bible from another Angle
- What Can I Do to Be A Better Church Member?

Book of the Bible Book Review

1. State the names of the main characters.

   a. Discuss their internal traits (including their ideas, prejudices, emotions, and ambitions).

   b. What factors were given to show how these personality traits were molded?

2. What is the setting?

3. What is the prevailing, or general, mood of the book: humorous, sad, despair, etc.? Explain why.

4. What is the writer's stated purpose for writing this book?

5. What is your personal reaction to the book?

6. What basic problem do the people face?

7. How do they manage to solve that problem or respond to that problem?

8. What main thought does the writer attempt to impress upon the reader?

9. What personal opinions or interests of the writer did you detect in the book?

10. What is/are the lesson/s that you learned from the book?

11. Summarize the book in your own words.

Sensory Images from Sensory Details

Use the senses to feel the words of the passage being read for deeper spiritual meaning.

Smell

Sight

Taste

Hearing

Touch (feeling)

Emotion (feeling)

Reading the Bible from another Angle

Use any of these ideas to enhance lesson development on specific passages. The suggestions that follow are not intended to be combined for one lesson.

1. Writing focus
   - How the passage is organized
   - How the writer elaborated ideas
   - The choice of words for the given context
     o Multiple meaning, situation, sensory images, similes, metaphors, dialogue
2. Type of writing
3. Types of sentences

   Statement, question, command
4. Sentence structure
   - Kinds of words that are used for particular functions
   - Subject—Who is doing something?
   - Predicate—What the subject is doing?
   - Noun—name, person, place, thing, idea
   - Verb—action, state that something is in existence (state of being)
   - Adjective/adverb—describes

(Just do not get too technical. Restrict the use of this strategy to what naturally flows from the passage. Do not force it.)

What Can I Do to Be a Better Church Member?

Read Hebrews 10:19–25 and then write your response.

1.

2.

3.

4.

5.

6.

7.

Appendix B

How Do You Teach a Bible Lesson to Assist Believers with Spiritual Growth?

Know what you are teaching and why you are teaching it.

Enrich the lesson.

Emphasize results—specific aims, goals, and objectives.

Be intentional about knowing the groundwork of each lesson for yourself.

Establish a baseline with personal study.

- Self-directed

- Continual

- Informed (in-home library, refresher readings, attend workshops)

  Evaluate yourself. (I recognize that I am a part of it rather than the center.)

  Pray in the classroom. (Do you use it only to open and close the session?)

Invite others to observe and critique you.

Plan for preparation

Evaluate your time management. (Is it effective?)

Evaluate your lesson planning. (Which part of the lesson is strongest/weakest?)

Use questions to stimulate discussion. (Do you write them down as part of your lesson plan?)

Review age appropriateness. (Are the activities right for the group?)

Consider positive and negative communication (verbal and nonverbal).

How Do You Teach a Bible Lesson to Assist Believers with Spiritual Growth?

Know how to draw the most out of believers with a variety of approaches.

Varied teaching techniques give the students multiple opportunities to use the lesson to help someone else.

Give them opportunities to share, participate, and implement their ideas.

Practical Application

Open the air for discussion.

games

role plays

displays

learning centers

technology

characters

simultaneous discussion teams (two to three persons)

aids—pictures, objects, or music that represent concepts

collect files—Lenten season, Advent, etc.

teachable moments—crises

Use questions and limit lecturing.

Performance Activities

Projects for all ages

Make it personal—take it home

Cooperative

Intergenerational

Service oriented

Appendix C

Survey Observations

During several seminars/workshops held between 1999 and 2001, I surveyed participants to find out their thoughts on a few ideas relating to Christian education. These results represent responses from urban and rural as well as small and larger churches throughout the state of Virginia. After compiling the comments from various surveys, it became clear to me that many people have different ideas about functions that religious organizations serve and roles various leaders play. Knowing the diversity of opinions held within the same organization has helped me to transform my approach as I continue to serve God.

I offer some suggestions that will assist in planning more effective ministries as a result of reviewing the responses. See if you can offer more ideas.

1. Give a variety of classes; offer a variety of styles of lesson presentation to encourage more adults, youth, and children to participate.

2. People are hungry for depth and want more time for class. Consider having fellowship opportunities where the lessons

can be continued over lunch one Saturday per quarter or coffee one evening when the group can meet in addition to the regular time.

3. Some of the lessons are boring because the teachers are last-minute preparers. It is difficult to motivate someone to do something that you are not willing to do yourself. Dynamic lessons take time to plan and workers meetings could highlight techniques for the lessons as well as the exegesis (definition and clarification) of the text.

4. Other _____

The bulleted lists that follow are verbatim survey responses.

What keeps you involved in the church?

- love
- love for Christ
- commitment to duty
- need to hear the Word
- fellowship with others; connect with other believers
- desire for spiritual growth
- spiritual empowerment

What can be done to prevent you from wanting to quit (involvement in a church)**?**

- never wanted to quit
- prayer and faith
- a deeper and abiding faith
- effective prayer for greater tolerance
- keeping prayed up and in the Word
- communication: talking to someone who has past experience

Describe the Duties of Sunday School Superintendents

- Organize activities, preside over Sunday school and/or a weekly Bible study and/or a weekly Bible study workers' meetings, and communicate with pastor and joint boards.
- Coordinate Sunday school and/or a weekly Bible study and/or a weekly Bible study classes, programs, fifty-nine to eighty members in Sunday school and/or a weekly Bible study and/or a weekly Bible study.
- Select teachers and teacher lesson plans.
- Be on time. Be in charge of the Sunday school and/or a weekly Bible study and/or a weekly Bible study as a whole.
- Lead the people; otherwise supervise (be in charge of meetings).

- Open Sunday school and/or a weekly Bible study and/or a weekly Bible study on time and remark short so lesson can be tougher.

- Act as the head person for correlating the teaching activities of the Sunday school and/or a weekly Bible study and/or weekly Bible study teachers.

- Guide new persons on what your duties are.

- Open the school; make sure the teachers are there.

- Try to teach and help teachers, to educate them on the Word of God and to develop Christian growth.

- Plan, organize, keep teachers informed, motivated, humble, and open to God's instructions.

- Coordinate the work of the Sunday school and/or a weekly Bible study and/or a weekly Bible study.

- Be overall in charge (under the pastor) of the Sunday school and/or a weekly Bible study and/or a weekly Bible study program and select and train teachers.

- Oversee smooth operation of the Sunday school and/or a weekly Bible study and/or a weekly Bible study, assist teachers when needed, promote the Sunday school and/or a weekly Bible study and/or a weekly Bible study.

Describe the Duties of Sunday School Union Presidents

- ➤ Preside over BTU meetings.

- ➤ Meet with other union presidents and plan with them what they anticipate doing for the year and agree with one another.

- ➤ Be the main person that gives information as to what should be done by the superintendents.

- ➤ Plan, coordinate, and conduct an annual BTU and Sunday school and/or a weekly Bible study and/or a weekly Bible study convention.

- ➤ Host two-day sessions during months with five Sundays with business and training workshops on Saturday and worship with host church on Sunday, available for training workshops throughout the year.

Describe the Duties of Association Leaders

- ⇨ Plan meetings, programs, etc.

- ⇨ Visit other churches and associations to see what they are doing.

- ⇨ Prepare for the association that meets each year for one or two days at different churches to listen to sermons, seminars, youth programs, etc. (the annual convention).

Note: Many areas do not have active regional bodies for training.

List your top five training needs.

1. **Training occurred in the majority of the responses.**

   - workshops that have a skilled, knowledgeable spirit-filled trainer that knows what they are really there for and teaching

   - even trained and spirit-led teachers need to be refreshed from time to time

   - willing persons that will come forth to be trained

   - group training—getting teachers together making sure they are teaching the same thing

   - equipping the superintendent to serve effectively, as well as the other church school officers

   - training teachers to be a teacher and getting them to attend lesson review sessions

   - teacher workshops—focusing on responsibilities as teachers of the Word

   - Sunday school and/or a weekly Bible study and/or a weekly Bible study training class and discussion of the lesson each week

   - training for superintendents so they can help the teachers/associates to be more effective teachers or leaders

- training or knowing what source of materials should be purchased
- training on effective vacation Bible school presentation
- train teachers to teach
- training the superintendent/leaders
- training in age-appropriate activities and how to discover your gifts in this particular area
- train teachers to use the Bible and reference materials
- superintendents need workshop training together
- training needed to let Sunday school and/or weekly Bible study members know that all teachers should be addressing the same lesson
- training others
- Scripture teaching and teachers training in presentation of the information

2. **The importance of Scripture was the second-most prevalent response.**

- stress importance of studying Scripture
- learning the Word of God
- how to apply the Word to our lives and the people we work with
- overall, let everyone know we must be trained and study God's Word in order to please God

- study Scripture at all times each and every day
- need improved methods of presenting the Scripture to the different age groups

3. **All other responses are listed with no particular hierarchy.**

- Understanding lesson so it can be explained to the class
- Give class assignments to bring to the group on the following Sunday
- We need to learn to stay in our area or function in your gift where we can remain effective and stop being legends in our own minds
- Ability to accept change
- Adequate space and materials
- I need ways to motivate teachers to attend Bible study and seminars
- How to use time more wisely
- Getting needed support from the pastoral staff
- To have more of a knowledge base on how to find "good" information
- How to get more class participation
- Productive responses
- Need to know how to motivate people in the doing of God's Word
- Better book for eight to fifteen age group

- Ways to motivate people
- Ways to get believers interested and study the Word
- Age-appropriate classes
- Chalkboards (portable), hands-on material, more training aids (bulletin boards, overhead projectors, videos)
- Planning classes for all youth teachers—three to ten age group
- Listening to what is asked and understanding it before you answer
- How to apply the lesson to today
- How to avoid arguing a point
- Being receptive to others' understanding or interpretation of the lesson
- Setting up the classroom for maximum effect/techniques
- How to improve my leadership skills
- Basic teaching skills—time management
- Bible interpretation and Baptist beliefs
- Discipline—maintaining order
- Teachers need to exercise their ability to keep the class (youth sixteen to twenty-three) focused on the Sunday school and/or a weekly Bible study lesson, getting rooted in the Word, making everyone feel like they are important (lesson review sessions)

- Teachers that are willing to teach, will study to teach, and will be on time
- More space in which to conduct classes (closed rooms to reduce distraction)
- Church leaders to attend Sunday school and/or a weekly Bible study (to set the example)
- Superintendents
- Program leaders
- Teach the children and also some adults how to stand when speaking
- Would like a method to make or cause Sunday school and/or a weekly Bible study to be more exciting
- Need the leaders of our church in Bible teaching and study to be more in the Word of God
- "I'm not going to that class"—not willing to "sit under his teaching"
- A teacher's assistant program
- All do same teaching
- Be able to talk to each other with the same voice from one day to another
- New or tried methods to involve quiet/don't like to talk individuals

Leader's Reflections Survey Results

How does the role of your group's leader effect and affect the growth of the Sunday school and the overall teaching ministry of the church?

- set the tone
- positive manner
- a great deal—when we lost our pastor due to death, the Sunday school and/or a weekly Bible study kept the faith
- improve Bible knowledge and understanding
- good
- I'm hopefully only a wheel in the middle of a hub
- make everyone aware that we can grow by faith
- there is little to no growth
- it's a priority

What does your group do that really works to enhance the growth of the Sunday school and/or a weekly Bible study?

- makes everyone feel a part of the group
- promotes participation
- evangelizes, recognizes those who have brought the most to Christ with dinner tickets
- allows believers to expand on the Word through individual expression

- learns how to take to the teacher

- plans programs—activities

- shows how to act toward one another

- Sunday school and/or a weekly Bible study promotion day held as well as promotion by superintendent on the fourth Sundays

How is that growth measured?

- participation and action

- believers become teachers

- quarterly evaluation

- participation

- by people participation

- by attendance

- by the attendance and the enthusiasm of the Sunday school and/or a weekly Bible study

- spirituality

How does your group motivate the participation of others?

- zeal brings on more zeal in others

- makes them feel

- assigns different responsibilities

- allows each student to express himself/herself

- by active participation

- little is done to motivate our Sunday school and/or a weekly Bible study
- encourages to use talents

What can your group do differently to stimulate greater participation of others?

- more outreach
- need to plan
- let them know they are much needed
- love and accept one another as Christ loved us
- the bringing together of the occupations
- let people have a chance to do something different
- be more active
- change some of the officers

What is God doing in your group or through your group?

- increasing knowledge and understanding
- taking us to new levels as growth allows
- letting us know he is in charge
- allowing the church to grow in his grace
- helping teachers to grow spiritually through learning to search the Scriptures
- teaching obedience
- showing us how to get along

What is wrong with your Sunday school and/or a weekly Bible study?

- not everyone has been reached

- needs to be promoted

- getting all to be on time and supporting in giving their monies

- not long enough to finish each lesson

- lack of teacher effectiveness

- not starting on time

- not enough adult participation

- I am not certain

- low attendance

What is right with your Sunday school and/or a weekly Bible study?

- teaching the Word with excitement

- willing leaders

- several good teachers

- lifts up our Lord and Savior Jesus Christ

- committed Christian members who continue to pray and support the Sunday school and/or a weekly Bible study

- the faithful few

- the length of time allocated (9:30–11:00)

- that we are blessed to have the ones we have

- Sunday school and/or a weekly Bible study and/or a weekly Bible study workers meetings monthly, pastor support

What are the challenges and issues you face with the Sunday school and/or a weekly Bible study?

- keeping the people stimulated
- pastor not attending
- aid teen mothers
- keeping everyone on one accord
- need for teachers and teacher training

What will your Sunday school and/or a weekly Bible study look like in the next millennium?

- even better with the help of the Lord
- looking to the Lord
- trusting God will help us where we need the help
- it is declining now; hopefully it will grow through the training in the Word
- I hope a 100 percent attendance rate
- crowded with love

Good servants minister what they have with servant love.

Points to Ponder

- What is happening in our churches if the leaders have difficulty articulating what it is that God is doing through them?

- What does the Bible say happens to a tree that does not bear good fruit? It seems that we are not sure what we are growing. (Matthew 4:8–10).
- God can raise up a stone. Don't let his ax cut down your tree.

Survey Conclusion

- The leaders need regular training sessions that will enable them to train others for evangelism, fulfilling the Great Commission.
- We need to be very intentional about demonstrating effective teaching techniques and resources that will reach the people where they are. They know what they need and we should feel an obligation to go and teach all of them wherever they are.
- There is a tremendous need for creative teaching techniques that will reach God's people in the future. Techniques are still being used that were innovative at the turn of the last century, 1900.
- Many people are crying out for help in revitalizing Christian education ministries. Approximately half of those who responded to the survey teach in their local church.
- Many leaders appear to be program oriented rather than ministry focused. Our leaders are very busy, but what are they

busy doing? Are they running an organization or meeting the needs of an organism?

- The leaders did not identify many things that they do that are measurable; the statements are vague.
- The leaders are not in consensus as to what the duties and responsibilities are of the superintendent, union presidents, and association leaders.
- Leaders are gathering people together but not equipping them to be scattered to do ministry beyond the doors of the church.

Endnotes

[1]   John Dewey. *Ethical Principles Underlying Education*. Chicago: University of Chicago Press, 1903, 31-32.

[2]   Jay Johnston, et al. *Teaching the Jesus Way: Building a Transformational Teaching Ministry*. Nashville: LifeWay Press, 2000, 121, 123–126, 140.

[3]   All references to Greek origins and scriptural definitions were taken from *The Hebrew-Greek Key Word Study Bible* edited by Spiros Zodhiates, 1998.

Photographed by Annette Riley, Ette' Photography,
April 2013. Used with permission.

Meet the Author

Barbara Arlene Fields Brehon

From an early age I found joy and inner peace at church, not understanding what it meant to serve the Lord. In my thirties I accepted God's call sitting on a beach at a retreat. While attending seminary, I recognized my call as equipping believers. It is like being a church body builder.

God majestically interweaves reading specialist and theological training into creatively sharing his Word. I've stumbled along, nevertheless, God uses it all for his glory. Practical experiences, encounters at retreats, workshops, conferences and churches are foundations for writing. Laboring for personal intimacy with the Lord, my passion is to share various topics that focus on helping others grow closer to God. I encourage you to recognize your purpose, know that God values you, and enjoy life in the love of Lord.

Currently residing in rural Tappahannock, Virginia, serving Beulah Baptist Church and Essex County Public Schools, I recently completed production of Beyond *Discipleship to Relationship: Developing Intimacy with the Lord,* slated for release in 2014. It complements *Reach Me with SMILES* and offers a practical, biblically sound approach for personal and corporate spiritual growth.